STRATEGIC COLLABORATIONS IN HEALTH SCIENCES LIBRARIES

AF795460

Chandos
Information Professional Series

Series Editor: Ruth Rikowski
(Email: rikowskigr@aol.com)

Chandos' new series of books is aimed at the busy information professional. They have been specially commissioned to provide the reader with an authoritative view of current thinking. They are designed to provide easy-to-read and (most importantly) practical coverage of topics that are of interest to librarians and other information professionals. If you would like a full listing of current and forthcoming titles, please visit www.chandospublishing.com.

New authors: We are always pleased to receive ideas for new titles; if you would like to write a book for Chandos, please contact Dr. Glyn Jones on g.jones.2@elsevier.com or telephone + 44 (0) 1865 843000.

STRATEGIC COLLABORATIONS IN HEALTH SCIENCES LIBRARIES

Edited by

JEAN P. SHIPMAN

M.J. TOOEY

ELSEVIER

CP
CHANDOS
PUBLISHING
An imprint of Elsevier

Chandos Publishing is an imprint of Elsevier
50 Hampshire Street, 5th Floor, Cambridge, MA 02139, United States
The Boulevard, Langford Lane, Kidlington, OX5 1GB, United Kingdom

Copyright © 2019 Jean P. Shipman and M.J. Tooey. Published by Elsevier Limited. All rights reserved.

No part of this publication may be reproduced or transmitted in any form or by any means, electronic or mechanical, including photocopying, recording, or any information storage and retrieval system, without permission in writing from the publisher. Details on how to seek permission, further information about the Publisher's permissions policies and our arrangements with organizations such as the Copyright Clearance Center and the Copyright Licensing Agency, can be found at our website: www.elsevier.com/permissions.

This book and the individual contributions contained in it are protected under copyright by the Publisher (other than as may be noted herein).

Notices
Knowledge and best practice in this field are constantly changing. As new research and experience broaden our understanding, changes in research methods, professional practices, or medical treatment may become necessary.

Practitioners and researchers must always rely on their own experience and knowledge in evaluating and using any information, methods, compounds, or experiments described herein. In using such information or methods they should be mindful of their own safety and the safety of others, including parties for whom they have a professional responsibility.

To the fullest extent of the law, neither the Publisher nor the authors, contributors, or editors, assume any liability for any injury and/or damage to persons or property as a matter of products liability, negligence or otherwise, or from any use or operation of any methods, products, instructions, or ideas contained in the material herein.

Library of Congress Cataloging-in-Publication Data
A catalog record for this book is available from the Library of Congress

British Library Cataloguing-in-Publication Data
A catalogue record for this book is available from the British Library

ISBN: 978-0-08-102258-0

For information on all Chandos Publishing publications visit our website at https://www.elsevier.com/books-and-journals

ELSEVIER Book Aid International
Working together to grow libraries in developing countries
www.elsevier.com • www.bookaid.org

Publisher: Glyn Jones
Acquisition Editor: Glyn Jones
Editorial Project Manager: Naomi Robertson
Production Project Manager: Swapna Srinivasan
Cover Designer: Mark Rogers

Typeset by TNQ Technologies

CONTENTS

CONTRIBUTORS

Aphrodite Bodycomb
Health Sciences and Human Services Library, University of Maryland, Baltimore, Baltimore, MD, United States

John Christian Tueller Bramble
National Network of Libraries of Medicine MidContinental Region, Spencer S. Eccles Health Sciences Library, University of Utah, Salt Lake City, UT, United States

Anna Brown
CEBIS Specialist, Library and Knowledge Services, University Hospitals Coventry and Warwickshire NHS Trust, Coventry, United Kingdom

Jamie Conklin
Health Sciences Library, University of North Carolina at Chapel Hill, Chapel Hill, NC, United States

Amber Dunlop
CEBIS Specialist, Library and Knowledge Services, University Hospitals Coventry and Warwickshire NHS Trust, Coventry, United Kingdom

Heidi Greenberg
Spencer S. Eccles Health Sciences Library, University of Utah, Salt Lake City, UT, United States

Patricia G. Hinegardner
Health Sciences and Human Services Library, University of Maryland, Baltimore, Baltimore, MD, United States

Megan von Isenburg
Medical Center Library & Archives, Duke University, Durham, NC, United States

Janice M. Jaguszewski
Health Sciences Libraries, University of Minnesota, Minneapolis, MN, United States

Christy Jarvis
Information Resources & Digital Initiatives, Spencer S. Eccles Health Sciences Library, University of Utah, Salt Lake City, UT, United States

Kyle Bradford Jones
Family and Preventive Medicine, University of Utah School of Medicine, Salt Lake City, UT, United States

Stephen Kiyoi
Library Director, ZSFG Library, UCSF, San Francisco, CA, United States

Erica Lake
Spencer S. Eccles Health Sciences Library, University of Utah, Salt Lake City, UT, United States

Leila Ledbetter
Medical Center Library & Archives, Duke University, Durham, NC, United States

Courtney Lyles
UCSF Division of General Internal Medicine, Zuckerberg San Francisco General Hospital, San Francisco, CA, United States

Robin L. Marcus
Department of Physical Therapy and Athletic Training, University of Utah, Salt Lake City, UT, United States
Office of Wellness and Integrative Health, University of Utah Health, Salt Lake City, UT, United States

Alexa Mayo
Health Sciences and Human Services Library, University of Maryland, Baltimore, Baltimore, MD, United States

Lisa A. McGuire
Health Sciences Libraries, University of Minnesota, Minneapolis, MN, United States

Gabriela Mircea
University Library, McMaster University, Hamilton, ON, Canada

Beverly Murphy
Medical Center Library & Archives, Duke University, Durham, NC, United States

Olga Perkovic
University Library, McMaster University, Hamilton, ON, Canada

Tracey Pratchett
Knowledge and Library Services Manager, Lancashire Teaching Hospitals NHS Foundation Trust, Preston, United Kingdom

J. Dale Prince
Louisiana State University Health Sciences Center, Division of Libraries, New Orleans, LA, United States

Shobha Sadasivaiah
UCSF School of Medicine, University of California, San Francisco, CA, United States

Jean P. Shipman
Global Library Relations, GSN, Elsevier, Cottonwood Heights, UT, United States
Spencer S. Eccles Health Sciences Library, University of Utah, Salt Lake City, UT, United States

Denise A. Smith
Health Sciences Library, Faculty of Health Sciences, McMaster University, Hamilton, ON, Canada

M.J. Tooey
Health Sciences and Human Services Library, University of Maryland, Baltimore, Baltimore, MD, United States

Victoria Treadway
Library and Knowledge Service Lead, Wirral University Teaching Hospital NHS Foundation Trust, Wirral, United Kingdom

Megan Van Noord
Medical Center Library & Archives, Duke University, Durham, NC, United States

Chris Lyle Wasden
Managing Partner of Digital Disruption Advisors, Midway, UT, United States

BIOGRAPHIES

Aphrodite Bodycomb

Aphrodite M. Bodycomb, MSM, MBA, is associate director for administration and operations at the University of Maryland's Health Sciences and Human Services Library (HSHSL). She has 25 years of combined management experience in the areas of administration, budgeting and finance, facilities, and information technology. Her strategic planning experience spans four organizations and includes experience in nonprofit, health-care, and corporate environments. Aphrodite previously served as vice chair of the University of Maryland Staff Senate, chair of the University System of Maryland Women's Forum, and is currently chair of the Innovation and Entrepreneurs Task Force at the HSHSL. Her bachelor of science degree focused on consumer economics and she has a master of science in management with a specialization in marketing and a master of business administration.

John Christian Tueller Bramble

John Christian Tueller Bramble, MLIS, began his career as a member of the University of Utah Spencer S. Eccles Health Sciences Library (EHSL) faculty in 2001. He has held a variety of positions during this time starting in reference and outreach services. In 2006, he began working on EHSL's contract with the National Library of Medicine to carry out the program of the National Network of Libraries of Medicine MidContinental Region (NNLM MCR). He has also held a variety of positions with the NNLM MCR, including interim associate director, resource sharing coordination and training, educational and communication technology training, and promoting and training on the librarian's role in supporting researchers at all points of the research lifecycle. For a short period, he shared a portion of his time managing the University of Utah Health U-Bar project. He specializes in educational and communication technologies and provides instruction on accessing quality/authoritative health-related online resources for all audience levels, from laypersons to biomedical researchers. He provides instruction to small and large groups, in-person or online synchronous/asynchronous classrooms, and self-directed online learning modules.

Anna Brown

Anna Brown, BA, MA, MCLIP, has been a Clinical Evidence Based Information System Specialist at University Hospitals Coventry and Warwickshire National Health Service (NHS) Trust in the United Kingdom since 2010, following a period working on NHS Evidence Specialist Collections at Warwick Medical School. She has also worked in academic and special libraries in the United Kingdom, Ireland, and New Zealand. She has an MA in information and library studies from Loughborough University, UK, and is a chartered member of the Chartered Institute of Library and Information Professionals, the UK's professional body for library and information professionals.

Jamie Conklin

Jamie Conklin, MSLIS, is a health sciences librarian at the University of North Carolina at Chapel Hill. She is also liaison to Nursing and a member of the steering of the committee for the Office of Interprofessional Education and Practice. She received her master's degree in library and information science from Florida State University. Her interests include evidence-based practice in nursing education, evidence-based teaching, interprofessional education, and open access to scholarly communication and instructional resources. She is a frequent visitor of her local public library and state parks.

Amber Dunlop

Amber Dunlop has been a clinical evidence based information system specialist at University Hospitals Coventry and Warwickshire National Health Service Trust since 2010. Prior to this, she spent almost 10 years working in a Postgraduate Medical Library, first as a library assistant and, after obtaining a National Vocational Qualification in Library and Information Studies, as a senior clinical library and information assistant leading the training program. She has a BA in cultural studies.

Heidi Greenberg

Heidi Greenberg is the Associate Director for Administration at the Spencer S. Eccles Health Sciences Library (EHSL) at the University of Utah. She was previously a research associate for EHSL and was the project lead for the U-Bar project. She has had the opportunity to present the U-Bar initiative to diverse groups within University of Utah Health and throughout other organizations in the country. Her past experience includes historical research projects for University of Utah Health and sleep research with Intermountain Life Flight, which received awards from the Association of Air Medical Services. She has a degree in business administration from Westminster College in Salt Lake City, Utah.

Patricia G. Hinegardner

Patricia G. Hinegardner, MLS, AHIP, is associate director for resources at the Health Sciences and Human Services Library (HSHSL), University of Maryland, Baltimore, where she provides leadership for the Resources Division, which includes Collection Strategies and Management, Resource Development and Sharing, and Metadata Management. She has worked at the HSHSL for over 30 years where she has held a variety of positions providing her with a broad perspective in librarianship. She has served as a reference librarian, liaison librarian to the School of Nursing, and web manager and has participated in several outreach projects. She has been the project leader on several grants and awards principally involving database development and digitization projects. She is a member of the Medical Library Association and a distinguished member of the Academy of Health Information Professionals. She has published articles, presented posters and has been active on professional committees.

Janice Jaguszewski

Janice Jaguszewski, MSLIS, is associate university librarian and director for the health sciences at the University of Minnesota. She and her colleagues in the Health Sciences Libraries are engaged in expanded services in evidence-based practice, systematic reviews, research impact measures, research workflow measures, and data management and curation. In addition, they are planning for a new library, which will be part of a Health Science Education Center to be built by early 2020. Services will include an Innovation Space, a Visualization Center, an Augmented and Virtual Reality Studio, and a Faculty Commons with an emerging technology sandbox. Janice has a passion for organization development (OD) and earned a certificate in OD through the University of Minnesota's College of Continuing Education. She focuses on coaching, strategic planning, and change management in her current position and has presented and consulted at a variety academic libraries including those at Penn State, Ohio State, the University of Texas, and the University of Saskatchewan. Janice has also published several articles on OD topics, including co-authoring a report for the Association of Research Libraries entitled, "New Roles for New Times: Transforming Liaison Roles in Research Libraries."

Christy Jarvis

Christy Jarvis, MLIS, AHIP, has worked in libraries in various capacities since 1998. She obtained her master of library and information science from San Jose State in 2004. She is currently the head of information resources and digital initiatives at the Spencer S. Eccles Health Sciences Library (EHSL), where she has been a member of the faculty since 2011. This role provides ample opportunity for her to initiate and foster collaborative relationships across the spectrum of scholarly publishing, both within the university and with external partners. As project lead for the EHSL's e-channel, she has been intimately involved in overcoming the challenges and celebrating the accomplishments of a publishing collaboration between the EHSL and the university's innovators and entrepreneurs. She is the author of several scholarly articles detailing the changing trends in information storage, retrieval, and dissemination and is the recipient of several research awards for investigating how these developments are impacting academic health sciences libraries.

Kyle Bradford Jones

Kyle Bradford Jones, MD, FAAFP, is an assistant professor (clinical) in the Department of Family and Preventive Medicine at the University of Utah School of Medicine. He graduated from residency in family medicine at the University of Utah in 2012, after graduating from the Medical College of Wisconsin in 2009. He has interest in how technology can improve patients' control over their own health. He also performs research on health-care costs and outcomes from novel ambulatory care delivery models. He practices at the Neurobehavior HOME Program, a patient-centered medical home for individuals with developmental disabilities. He enjoys personal time with his wife and four children.

Stephen Kiyoi

Stephen Kiyoi, MLIS, MS HAIL, AHIP, is director of the University of California, San Francisco (UCSF) Library at Zuckerberg San Francisco General, and a co-principal investigator for the National Library of Medicine (NLM) G08 Grant to engage patients in using online patient portals for health-care management. Before joining UCSF, Stephen was an associate fellow at the NLM, where he worked on user interface design, outreach to special populations, and legislative advocacy. Stephen received his master of library and information science degree from the University of California, Los Angeles (UCLA), and master's in health-care administration and interprofessional leadership from UCSF. He is past president of the

Northern California and Nevada Medical Library Group. Stephen was an NLM/Association of Academic Health Sciences Libraries (AAHSL) leadership fellow (2015–16) and has received awards for Showcased Final Portfolio (UCLA MLIS), Best Overall Evidence-Based Capstone Project (UCSF MS HAIL), Best Capstone Project Paper (UCSF MS HAIL), Leadership Scholarship (AAHSL), and the Professional Development Award (MLA LMS). He has published on the topics of patient portal engagement, leadership development in librarianship, and library outreach to special populations.

Erica Lake

Erica Lake, MLS, AHIP, joined the faculty at the Spencer S. Eccles Health Sciences Library at the University of Utah in 2011 as an associate librarian and associate director of the Hope Fox Eccles Health Library. In this role, she provides consumer health information services for the University of Utah Health system, the University of Utah campus, and the greater Salt Lake Valley community. She earned her MLS at Indiana University and has worked in academic, public, and special libraries. Throughout her 16-year medical library career, she has worked to create gateways for consumers and clinicians to access evidence-based health-care information and has taken leadership roles in coordinating organizationwide availability of online resources. She is currently involved in a wide range of projects and initiatives with clinicians, bioinformaticists, university faculty, public librarians, community partners, and local organizations. These include researching the effect health information provision has on patient outcomes and engagement, building organizational patient education information infrastructure, and integrating library services into the electronic health record and patient portal.

Leila Ledbetter

Leila Ledbetter, MLIS, is a research and education librarian with the Duke University Medical Center Library. She received her master of library and information science degree from the School of Information Studies, University of Wisconsin at Milwaukee and has a BS in biology from Marietta College in Marietta, Ohio. She is the library liaison for the Doctor of Physical Therapy program and the Master of Biomedical Sciences program, as well as the Duke Area Health Education Center program. As a research specialist, she works with faculty, students and medical center staff on everything from systematic reviews of the literature to conference posters. Her professional interests include systematic reviews of the literature, learning theory, and evidence-based medicine.

Courtney Lyles

Courtney Lyles, PhD, is an assistant professor in the University of California, San Francisco (UCSF) Division of General Internal Medicine at Zuckerberg San Francisco General Hospital, an associate faculty member at the UCSF Center for Vulnerable Populations, and an affiliate investigator at the Kaiser Permanente Northern California Division of Research. She received a PhD in health services from the University of Washington. She is currently principal investigator of a career development award from the Agency for Healthcare Research and Quality and co-principal investigator of a G08 grant from the National Library of Medicine to engage patients in using online patient portals for health-care management. As a health services researcher with both quantitative and qualitative expertise, her research focuses on harnessing health information technology to improve patient–provider communication for chronic disease self-management to ultimately reduce disparities in health and health-care outcomes. She has led several studies evaluating the impact of health technology on quality and clinical outcomes, as well as conducted extensive work with diverse patients to understand usability needs and preferences in using health technologies, both in clinical settings and in their everyday lives.

Robin Marcus

Robin Marcus, PT, PhD, is a professor of physical therapy and the chief wellness officer (CWO) for University of Utah Health. She is interested in the transformation of health care and of the responsibility that health-care professionals have in helping to find solutions to the health and wellness challenges of our community. Her interest also includes the responsibility for the health system's focus on faculty and staff well-being and resilience. In her current role, she is exploring the continuum of wellness and rehabilitation services that contribute to improved quality of life for healthy individuals and for those living with chronic health conditions. In addition to her role as the CWO, she currently serves the University as the associate dean for clinical affairs for the College of Health, the director of the L.S. Skaggs Patient Wellness Center, and as an advisory member for the Health Sciences Resiliency Center and Graduate Medical Education Wellness committee. She is also active in local, regional and national wellness initiatives as a steering committee member of *Get Healthy Utah*, on the board of directors of *Girls on the Run Utah*, and on the Evidence-Based Practice committee of the national organization, *Building Healthy Academic Communities*.

Alexa Mayo

Alexa Mayo, MLS, AHIP, is associate director for services at the Health Sciences and Human Services Library (HSHSL), University of Maryland, Baltimore, where she provides leadership for the public service departments within the library: Research, Education, and Outreach Services; Information Services; and Bioinformation Services. She has served in the position since 2005 and in public service positions at the HSHSL beginning in 1994, first as liaison librarian to the School of Medicine and then as assistant director. She has extensive experience in a variety of library settings, having worked in general academic, special, hospital, and the HSHSL, a large, publicly funded academic health sciences library. She is active in the Medical Library Association (MLA) and in MLA's Mid-Atlantic Chapter (MAC). In 2013–14, Alexa was a fellow in the National Library of Medicine/Association of Academic Health Sciences Librarians Leadership Fellows Program. While at the HSHSL, she has managed six funded projects, several of them multiyear projects with community partners. She writes and presents on her professional expertise and experience in developing innovative research support services and in global and community outreach.

Lisa McGuire

Lisa McGuire, MLIS, is associate director for education and research services for the Health Sciences Libraries at the University of Minnesota. She focuses on leading, shaping, and overseeing a department with responsibilities for campus engagement, research services, teaching and learning, content and collections management, and outreach activities. Lisa actively engages in mentoring and developing the knowledge, skills, and abilities of the nine professional liaison librarians in her department.

Gabriela Mircea

Gabriela Mircea, BSc, MISt, is the digital repository librarian at McMaster University, Hamilton, Ontario, Canada. One of her main tasks is to build and maintain a sophisticated technical infrastructure supporting the campus community in ingesting and archiving McMaster's myriad digital collections. Over the years, she has built a thorough and in-depth knowledge of scholarly communication finding digital preservation a very engaging aspect of the digital environment.

Beverly Murphy

Beverly Murphy, MLS, AHIP, FMLA, is assistant director for communications and web content management at the Duke University Medical Center Library and Archives and the hospital nursing liaison for the Duke Health System and Watts School of Nursing. As the liaison, she works with nursing faculty, staff, and students—teaching and assisting with their research needs for publication, quality improvement, performance evaluation, graduate residency, and class assignments. She has been at Duke for 35 years and is an alumnus of North Carolina Central University in Durham, NC, where she received a BS in biology and a master's in library science. Beverly is a distinguished member of the Medical Library Association's (MLA) Academy of Health Information Professionals and has served in a variety of capacities for the association, including president-elect, MLA news editor, MLA fellow, and member of the editor board of the *Journal of the Medical Library Association*. She is also active in the Mid-Atlantic Chapter of MLA and the Association of North Carolina Health and Science Libraries. Her research interests include electronic health record and Infobutton technology, librarian core competencies, diversity and inclusion in libraries, reference management, and library administration. She has co-authored journal articles, a book chapter, posters, and given presentations. She is currently co-editing a book, *Diversity & Inclusion in Libraries: A Changing Facet of Librarianship*, which is due for publication in early 2019.

Olga Perkovic

Olga Perkovic, MLIS, is the research and advanced studies librarian at McMaster University, Hamilton, Ontario, Canada. In this position, she works with faculty, graduate students, and other researchers to provide support for all phases of the research and scholarly process. She helps manage MacSphere, McMaster's institutional repository, and the library's two, open access journal publishing platforms, i.e., McMaster University Library Press and Student Journals@McMaster University. She works closely with campus partners such as the School of Graduate Studies, providing services and support for McMaster students and researchers. She actively promotes open access for research and education and has collaborated with colleagues in other institutions to create open resources.

Tracey Pratchett

Tracey Pratchett, MA, PGCE, MCLIP, has worked in the health sector for 10 years as both a clinical librarian and the knowledge and library services manager at Lancashire Teaching Hospitals National Health Service Foundation Trust. She is the joint project lead for the MAP (Making Alignment a Priority) community of practice (https://maptoolkit.wordpress.com) and is also interested in developing services and innovation across organizational boundaries. She jointly leads the Service Transformation eLearning Project (https://www.e-lfh.org.uk/programmes/literature-searching/) and was a former member of the Knowledge for Healthcare Metrics Working Group. She is passionate about sharing learning and developing herself and others through both informal and formal networks.

J. Dale Prince

J. Dale Prince, MA, MLS, AHIP, is director of libraries at the Louisiana State University Health Sciences Center in New Orleans. Previously, he was executive director of the National Network of Libraries of Medicine, Southeastern Atlantic Region. He received his BA and MA in English from the University of Alabama and his MLS from Indiana University. He has a keen interest in technology and its use to provide service and outreach to health information users. Sharing this interest, he has written many articles explaining new and emerging technologies for a librarian audience.

Shobha Sadasivaiah

Shobha Sadasivaiah, MD, MPH, is an assistant professor at the University of California, San Francisco, School of Medicine, and the patient portal physician champion. She is an internist at Zuckerberg San Francisco General Hospital and received her medical degree at Weill Cornell Medical College and her MPH at the University of California, Berkeley. She completed her residency training in internal medicine at the University of California, San Francisco. Her area of interest is in clinical informatics, specifically on technology use in vulnerable populations to improve health.

Jean P. Shipman

Jean P. Shipman, MSLS, AHIP, FMLA, is vice president, Global Library Relations for Elsevier. Prior to that, she was the executive director, knowledge management and Spencer S. Eccles Health Sciences Library; director of the MidContinental Region and National Training Office of the National Network of Libraries of Medicine; director for Information Transfer, Center of Medical Innovation; and adjunct faculty of the

Department of Biomedical Informatics, School of Medicine, all at the University of Utah. She has also been employed by the John Hopkins University; the Greater Baltimore Medical Center; the University of Maryland, Baltimore; the University of Washington; and Virginia Commonwealth University. She served as president of the Medical Library Association from 2006 to 2007 and on the board of directors for the Society for Scholarly Publishing from 2013 to 2016. She was a member and co-chair of the Chicago Collaborative, a group of publishers, librarians and editors, who met to discuss issues regarding scholarly communications. She is the co-editor of two books: *Information and Innovation: A Natural Combination for Health Sciences Libraries*, and this book, *Strategic Collaborations in Health Sciences Libraries*. She has also authored many journal articles, book chapters and given numerous professional presentations.

Denise Smith

Denise Smith, MLIS, is an education liaison librarian at the Health Sciences Library at McMaster University in Hamilton, Ontario, Canada. Before joining McMaster in 2014, she was a liaison librarian at Brock University in St Catharines, Ontario. She served as president of the Ontario College and University Library Association in 2016 and currently sits on the International Federation of Library Association's Information Literacy Standing Committee. She has many professional interests, including digital citizenship, open access scholarship, and metaliteracy. In 2018 she was accepted as a PhD candidate in library and information science at Western University. Her personal interests include ballet, knitting, and being outside.

M.J. Tooey

Mary Joan (M.J.) Tooey, MLS, AHIP, FMLA, is associate vice president, academic affairs and executive director of the Health Sciences and Human Services Library at the University of Maryland where she has worked in various library positions since 1986. She is also the director of the National Network of Libraries of Medicine's Southeastern Atlantic Regional Medical Library and the National DOCLINE Coordinating Office under a cooperative agreement with the National Library of Medicine at National Institutes of Health. She received her MLS from the University of Pittsburgh.

Tooey served as president of the Medical Library Association (2005–06), is a distinguished member of the Academy of Health Information Professionals, and a fellow of the Association. In 2016, she was the Medical Library Association's Janet Doe Lecturer. In 1997, she was named the Estelle Brodman Academic Medical Librarian of the Year. She has also served as president of the Association of Academic Health Sciences Libraries (2012–13). She was the 2011 recipient of the Distinguished Alumni Award from the University of Pittsburgh's School of Information Sciences. Tooey is the author or co-author of over 200 chapters, articles, presentations, or posters. Her professional interests include leadership, emerging trends, strategic planning and visioning, library innovation and design, ethics, and mentoring.

Victoria Treadway

Victoria Treadway, MA, MCLIP, has worked in health libraries since 2004, including 6 years as a clinical librarian, and is currently the library and knowledge service lead at Wirral University Teaching Hospital National Health Service Foundation Trust in the North West of England. She works alongside health-care professionals and teams to understand their knowledge requirements and deliver accessible and responsive library services. She is the joint lead of the MAP (Making Alignment a Priority) toolkit and is currently undertaking research to explore the role of the embedded librarian in supporting health-care professionals, patients and families in Critical Care.

Megan Van Noord

Megan Van Noord, MSIS, is a research and education librarian at the Duke Medical Center Library and Archives and the Liaison to the School of Medicine at Duke University. She received her master's degree in information science and certificate in interdisciplinary health communication from the University of North Carolina at Chapel Hill. Megan's research interests include systematic review methodology, teaching evidence-based practice, and bibliometrics. She has conducted peer review for the *Journal of Clinical Epidemiology*, *BMC*, and the *Journal of Affective Disorders*.

Megan von Isenburg

Megan von Isenburg, MSLS, AHIP, is associate dean for the Medical Center Library and Archives. She received her BA in American studies and her master's degree in library science from the University of North Carolina at Chapel Hill. Megan's research interests are medical education, evidence-based practice, and global health. She has served as co-director for the School of Medicine's Evidence Based Medicine (EBM) course and for the Duke Teaching and Leading EBM workshop. As liaison to Graduate Medical Education, Megan has participated in morning reports and noon conference across disciplines.

Chris Lyle Wasden

Chris Lyle Wasden, MBA, is the Managing Partner of Digital Disruption Advisors in Midway, Utah. PhD, Formerly he was the executive director of the Sorenson Center for Discovery & Innovation at the David Eccles School of Business at the University of Utah. Previously he served as a managing director at PricewaterhouseCoopers and its Global Healthcare Innovation Leader. As a global thought leader, he has authored over 60 articles, chapters, and books on innovation and digital health. His latest book *Tension—The Energy of Innovation* describes how individuals and organizations become more innovative by riding the Innovation Cycle along the entire Innovation Lifecycle. He advises leading companies on the Internet of Things and how social, mobile, analytics, and cloud technologies are transforming industries and business models, creating a culture of innovation, and developing new market opportunities. He is a named inventor on 11 issued patents and has been a leader in 10 different startups where he developed many of his ideas around the innovation cycle and lifecycle, and how fast, frequent, frugal, and failure accelerates innovation. He has a doctorate in human and organizational learning from George Washington University in Washington, DC, an MBA from the University of California, Los Angeles, Anderson School, and bachelor degrees in accounting (BS) and Asian studies (BA) from Brigham Young University in Provo, Utah.

PREFACE

WHY?

Why is there a need for a book on collaborations in health sciences libraries? With collaboration, there are characteristics of equality, creativity, and mutual benefit. For these reasons, collaboration and collaborative projects are positive and valuable to institutions and organizations, and especially to libraries. In health sciences libraries, there are great opportunities—financially, strategically, and even politically—to advance the work, not only of the institution, but of the library. Collaborations raise library visibility by beginning, sustaining, and advancing partnerships and teams that might never have existed. With a sense of shared purpose and common goals, success is important to all members of the collaboration team. Collaborations educate library partners as to the skills, abilities, and expertise of library teams.

In the health sciences, collaboration is especially relevant whether in a hospital library, national health services, or academic health sciences setting. Health sciences libraries, whatever their setting, are focused simply on health. This singularity of purpose evidences itself at the bedside, in the laboratory, in the community, and in the classroom. The focus could be on clinical care, research, administration, and supporting the intellectual growth of faculty and students. There is a place for health sciences libraries in all these settings. In health sciences libraries, collaboration can occur, not only within institutions but also across institutions separated by miles and mission, in communities, or even among individuals focused on improving the human condition by improving themselves, their libraries, and their professional practice.

BOOK OVERVIEW

The chapters selected for *Strategic Collaborations in Health Sciences Libraries* illustrate the key points made above. The wide variety of topics are inspirational in their creativity and passion for the collaborative work being performed. Furthermore, they shed light on the myriad skills librarians bring to the table—from chapters addressing financial collaborations to ones focused on building teams to improve care. There are chapters that advance collaborations with innovators, not only institutionally but also nationally and globally, and ones using collaborations to improve communities. Collaborations can support the library itself through strategic planning or envisioning a new space or interlibrary partnerships. These chapters involve all kinds of library staff as well—from library directors to library front-line staff—to staff peripheral to libraries.

The shared wealth of ideas and expertise is amazing, as are the creative solutions to many of the challenges faced in collaborating. No one said collaborations are easy. Many of the chapters address stumbling blocks and setbacks and include solutions, workarounds, lessons learned, and illustrate perseverance. There are case studies of successful collaborations where librarians were problem-solvers, initiators, leaders, facilitators, or promoters of collaborations within their libraries, institutions, communities, and beyond.

FROM THE EDITORS

The editors encourage readers to reflect on the examples provided in the chapters to identify, apply, or adapt the great processes, techniques, and lessons learned to local needs and situations. Seeking collaborations with others can ensure future success. Comments about the book, as well as other collaborative ideas, are welcomed by the editors. Let this book be the foundation for meaningful conversations regarding effective and creative collaborations. Meanwhile, enjoy the content. Collaborate with intention, dedication, and purpose—enriching and expanding knowledge and expertise.

CHAPTER 1

CEBIS: Collaborating With Clinicians to Inform Evidence-Based Practice

Amber Dunlop, Anna Brown
CEBIS Specialist, Library and Knowledge Services, University Hospitals Coventry and Warwickshire NHS Trust, Coventry, United Kingdom

INTRODUCTION

Evidence-Based Health Care

The evidence-based health-care movement has from the beginning identified itself as the integration of the best available research evidence with individual clinical expertise, including the "thoughtful identification and compassionate use of individual patients' predicaments, rights, and preferences in making clinical decisions about their care,"[1] as illustrated in Fig. 1.1. In many health-care settings, librarians or information professionals use their discovery and appraisal skills to identify the best available evidence. The clinician and the patient must not be forgotten. To best support the

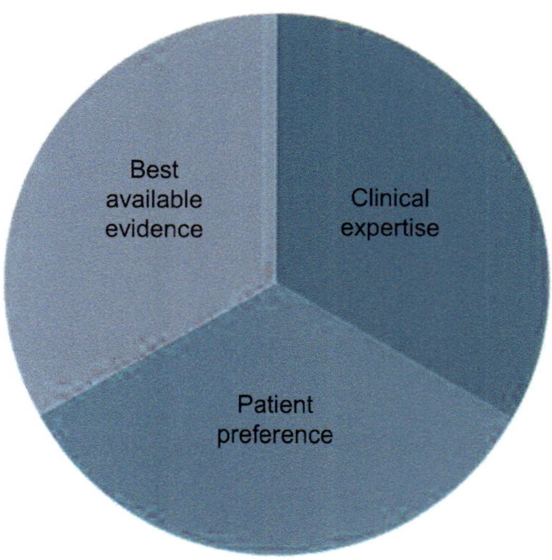

Figure 1.1 The essential components of evidence-based health care.

Strategic Collaborations in Health Sciences Libraries
ISBN 978-0-08-102258-0
https://doi.org/10.1016/B978-0-08-102258-0.00001-X
Copyright © 2019 Jean P. Shipman and M.J. Tooey. Published by Elsevier Limited. All rights reserved.

clinical decision-making process, evidence reviews need to be provided in a timely manner at the point of care, should take into account the complexity and concerns of individual patients, and encourage clinical input and questioning of the evidence with regard to its applicability to the situation at hand. Through close collaboration with clinical staff, information professionals can better understand and meet the needs of clinicians and their patients.

Setting

The National Health Service (NHS) in England is one of the four publicly funded national health-care services of the United Kingdom (NHS England, NHS Scotland, NHS Wales, and Health and Social Care in Northern Ireland). Established together in 1948, they provide comprehensive health services, free at the point of delivery, for residents of the United Kingdom. NHS England is a vast public body, comprising many different smaller organizations serving specific geographical areas and/or functions (e.g., acute care, primary care, mental health care, or ambulance services).

University Hospital in Coventry, central England, is an acute teaching hospital, and one of the largest such hospitals in the country. The hospital serves a population of over 1,000,000 people, employs over 8000 members of staff delivering care to 1100 patient beds, and has 26 operating theaters on site.[2]

The library at University Hospital, staffed by a mix of professional and paraprofessional staff, provides access to thousands of print and electronic books and journals, searchable electronic databases, physical space with computers, professional expertise, and information skills training. These services are available to all hospital employees, as well as affiliated students, supporting them in all areas of their work or study, including research, evidence-based practice, teaching, and learning.

DEVELOPMENT OF CLINICAL EVIDENCE BASED INFORMATION SERVICE

History of Clinical Evidence Based Information Service

In 2004, a Clinical Librarian (CL) service, consisting of one librarian, was implemented at the University Hospital. The CL developed the Evidence in Practice Group (EPG) model of delivering the best available evidence. EPGs involved the CL working collaboratively with a clinician to enable unbiased critical appraisal of evidence to be applied at a local level, then presenting this to the relevant clinical team to stimulate clinical discussion and the implementation of the evidence into practice. The role of the CL was to use critical appraisal skills and neutral viewpoint to present the evidence in an unbiased way in an environment where clinicians may be happier to practice based on the opinion that they have "been doing it that way for years." Working closely with a clinician ensured the request for evidence had been properly understood and the evidence was applicable to the local setting/population. The CL also worked with a member of the Information Technology (IT) department to develop a pilot IT system.

In 2006, a business case was presented for additional CL posts, alongside further development of the IT system. The case was presented by the Head of Knowledge Services, as the manager with responsibility for the hospital library, its services, and staff. At that time the hospital's board of executives declined the request. By 2009, the case showing the need for further investment grew based on the success of the CL service. A second business case was presented for the service now named the Clinical Evidence Based Information Service (CEBIS). On this occasion, the Head of Knowledge Services was successful in securing funding from three of the five clinical divisions for three full-time equivalent CEBIS specialists to work within the specialties covered by those divisions. Three CEBIS specialist posts have been in place since 2010. In 2012, as a result of the reorganization of clinical divisions into smaller groups of specialties, the CEBIS specialists are now centrally funded and free to work with staff from across the hospital. The 2009 business case also secured funding for the in-house development of an IT system with the capability to link directly to the electronic patient record.

Purpose and Aims of the Clinical Evidence Based Information Service

CEBIS builds on the CL model of delivering evidence at the point of care. CEBIS promotes the use of research evidence in practice by providing the information to facilitate evidence-based decision-making in a timely and effective manner. The primary aim of CEBIS is to collaborate with clinical staff to support quality patient care, either by aiding decision making about an individual patient's care, or improving evidence-based practice more broadly by working on research and audit projects, development of local guidelines or through advancement of professional knowledge. CEBIS is staffed by three qualified and experienced information specialists and supported by an IT system linked directly to the electronic patient health record. This enables colleagues to make requests for evidence as routinely as if making a referral for a blood test or X-ray. Requests to CEBIS are therefore termed "referrals," embodying the integration of an evidence search and discussion in the patient care process.

The Service and How It Works

CEBIS referrals may be submitted via a web form linked to the dedicated IT system, in person to the CEBIS specialist, by phone or email, or via the electronic patient record. For referrals relating to an individual patient, the latter option allows the CEBIS specialists to identify the patient and read relevant clinical notes shedding more light onto the clinical problem, as well as providing documentation of consultation of the research evidence alongside that patient's notes. CEBIS specialists, regarded as a member of a patient's clinical team, attend the same training and agree to the same policies as clinical staff regarding access to the patient record. They are trusted to access information about patients in accordance with information governance policies and data protection regulations. Search results, evidence summaries, presentations, and any discussion associated with each referral are stored on the searchable IT system.

The three CEBIS specialists are each aligned with specialty groups with whom they work particularly closely. The aim is to work in an embedded way as a member of the clinical team, attending ward rounds, clinics or clinical meetings, thereby contributing information and knowledge to improve day-to-day patient management. Being present in a clinical area also encourages the asking of questions and seeking of evidence by clinicians as uncertainties arise, rather than allowing these to go unanswered as a result of time pressures. The case studies provide examples of embedded working.

CEBIS referrals arising from nonembedded specialties are allocated to team members according to workload. While each specialist manages their own work, the team shares an office and often discusses searches or referrals to obtain advice or suggestions from colleagues. Training and skills development in areas such as critical appraisal and advanced searching are largely undertaken internally. This is a collaborative approach, with much sharing of knowledge and experience between the members of both CEBIS and other staff at the hospital library, including a knowledge skills librarian and electronic resources librarian.

CASE STUDIES

Neonatology

Analysis of Referrals

University Hospital delivers specialist neonatal care to newborn infants from 23 weeks gestational age through the Neonatal Intensive Care Unit (NICU). The NICU multidisciplinary care team was involved in the pilot year of CEBIS development, inviting a CEBIS specialist to attend weekly multidisciplinary team grand rounds on the ward. This working relationship has flourished over time and each week CEBIS provides evidence to inform clinical practice, supporting clinical staff in delivering EPGs and facilitating clinical discussions to enhance evidence-based practice, education, and service development.

In 2017, the CEBIS specialist undertook a review of CEBIS referrals submitted by the NICU team assessing the impact of an information specialist during teaching grand rounds, and providing a detailed account of how and where the impact was felt most. A full breakdown of these referrals by purpose can be seen in Fig. 1.2. During this period, members of the NICU team made a total of 265 evidence referrals, across all disciplines.

Having a dedicated information professional in attendance at weekly grand rounds has resulted in better use of evidence at the point of care. The NICU team regularly uses CEBIS to question current practice, inform parents of likely outcomes for their infants or in some cases choices of treatment options, educate multidisciplinary staff, update clinical guidelines, stimulate clinical discussions, develop new services, and confirm best practice.

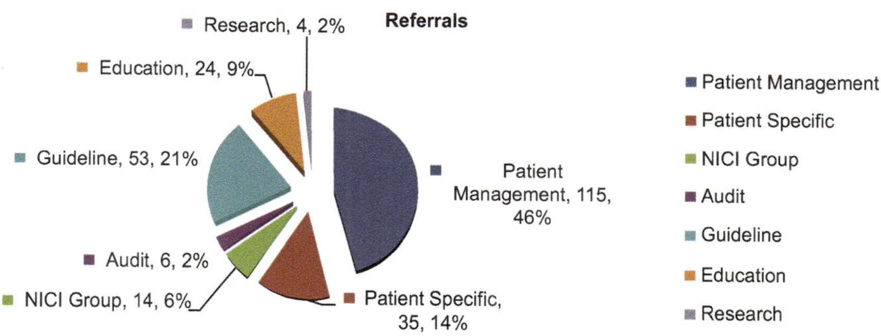

Figure 1.2 CEBIS referrals made by the NICU team—2013 to 2017.

Neonatal Infection Control and Improvement

The Neonatal Infection Control and Improvement (NICI) team, a multidisciplinary task group, was established in response to an infection outbreak on the NICU. The CEBIS specialist was invited to join the team to provide the best available evidence to change practice and lower rates of infection. The collaboration led to the following evidence-based changes:

- A change from a higher concentration to 0.2% chlorhexidine skin cleansing solution applied at the site of vascular access to avoid burns on extremely preterm skin while still efficiently eradicating risk of infection.
- The development of a fully evidence-based ventilator-associated pneumonia care bundle, including best practice in diagnosis and management of the condition to reduce rates of severe infection in ventilated infants.
- A change in use of fixation devices to reduce injury in neonates requiring endotracheal tubes.
- A comparison of efficacy of continuous versus intermittent administration of vancomycin in neonates resulting in a change in the way vancomycin is administered.

The NICI team continues to meet regularly, with the CEBIS specialist providing evidence on topics such as creating boundaries around incubator spaces to limit the contact with potentially contaminated materials.

Ophthalmology

The Department of Ophthalmology is a large multidisciplinary department of around 150 staff providing comprehensive ophthalmology care. The outpatient throughput is approximately 80,000 patients per year, and surgical throughput is over 5000 surgical procedures per annum. Ophthalmology staff are long-time supporters of CEBIS and are one of the biggest users of library services at University Hospital.

As Ophthalmology is primarily clinic and theater-based, with no dedicated wards, CEBIS specialist involvement "on the ground" is mainly through attendance at meetings dedicated to evidence-based practice, teaching and learning, and/or discussion of interesting cases. Attendance at clinics has been useful to learn about regularly encountered conditions, as well as picking up queries arising in this setting. However, on a long-term basis, attendance at clinics was found not to be the best use of CEBIS time. The CEBIS specialist is a regular presence in the department, and clinicians have her contact details, so requests for evidence that arise in clinics are usually raised in a timely manner. In addition to collaborating with clinicians for the purpose of direct patient care, the CEBIS specialist also provides information to support research projects, journal publications, and conference presentations.

CEBIS collaborates particularly closely with the vitreoretinal subspecialty team, which holds a weekly EPG. The CEBIS specialist is regarded as a member of the team and is welcomed for skills in accessing the evidence and for bringing a different perspective free of the inherent biases of being immersed in the clinical environment.

Patient Information

Two CEBIS EPGs with the vitreoretinal team have resulted in the creation of new patient information leaflets. Evidence on the management of both acquired retinoschisis and epiretinal membrane suggested that in many cases, no treatment, or "watchful waiting," may present no more risk to vision than surgical intervention. Experienced clinicians had found that many patients expect intervention and have high expectations regarding the outcomes of surgery. A need for evidence-based patient information for both conditions was identified. Both leaflets were drafted by the CEBIS specialist following discussion at EPG and brought back to the clinical team for further review and editing.

Audit Projects

The CEBIS specialist has supported many audit projects undertaken by Ophthalmology junior doctors, by providing information to benchmark performance against other centers or by identifying research gaps in the literature to be addressed by a project. One such audit looked at how effectively patients with suspected intraocular melanoma were managed, as speedy referral to a specialist ocular oncology center is of paramount importance in these cases. The CEBIS specialist was able to identify national guidelines providing referral timescales, as well as research addressing the accuracy and speed of referral to expert centers, including the effects of delays in treatment. When the audit identified that the protocol for referring patients with suspected intraocular melanoma was not as clear and well known by clinicians as it should be, the CEBIS specialist again collaborated with the junior doctors, helping create a hospital guideline and pro forma for referral to Liverpool Ocular Oncology Centre. The CEBIS specialist ensured the new guidance was made available to all staff as quickly as possible through the institutional intranet and document management system. This will hopefully improve the speed of referral to specialist centers in future.

Hospital Guidelines, Protocols, and Procedures

CEBIS specialists often work with clinicians in ensuring hospital guidelines and protocols follow the most up-to-date and best available evidence, appropriate to local conditions and patients. CEBIS supports both reviews of existing guidelines and the creation of new ones when needed. Working closely with Ophthalmology over a period of 7 years has led to the CEBIS specialist becoming familiar with Departmental guidelines and the evidence upon which they are based. The guideline for endophthalmitis, a serious, potentially eye-threatening infection, is one on which both the CEBIS specialist and the previous CL have been consulted many times on various aspects of the best possible management of a suspected case. This includes the use of the oral antibiotic linezolid because of its superior penetration into the vitreous, which the team believes has led to excellent outcomes in several endophthalmitis cases and avoided the need for supplementary antibiotic injections into the eye itself.[3]

The CEBIS specialist monitors the literature on endophthalmitis, and when the latest version of a European guideline[4] recommended consideration of intravitreal steroid injection, an EPG was organized to look into the possible benefits of this. However, the evidence was inconclusive, as supported by a recent Cochrane review.[5] Correspondence with the author of an unpublished trial in the Netherlands supported nonuse of the intravitreal steroid. This recommendation was therefore not added to the local guideline.

CHALLENGES

Clinician Time Limitations

The NHS is "facing unprecedented financial and operational pressures, with many NHS organizations in deficit and key performance standards being missed."[6] This is a result of increasing demand for health care, unmatched by increases in funding for health or social care.[7] Staff shortages mean clinician time is limited. Finding the opportunity to visit the library or search clinical databases is no longer a priority, and in some cases, is not even a possibility.

Through flexible collaborative working, CEBIS specialists support clinicians in making the best use of their time. Embedded information specialists are able to clarify clinical questions at the time and place best suited to clinical teams, regularly participating in clinics and grand rounds to get a complete clinical picture without having to interrupt clinicians during their busiest times. Specialists are able to conduct searches either within the clinical setting or from their office, working to meet user deadlines and delivering tailored evidence summaries with seamless access to full-text papers wherever possible, thus removing a time and financial barrier to full review of the evidence. CEBIS Specialists stop short of preparing their own summaries of clinical studies, believing that this risks introducing unintentional bias, and full papers are better reviewed by the decision-maker with clinical expertise, albeit in conjunction with an information professional who may advise on study methodology or validity. Clinicians are able to submit referrals 24/7 via email, web forms, or directly via the electronic individual patient record. This removes the need for clinicians to attend the library or call their specialist to explain their evidence needs.

While CEBIS undoubtedly saves time for clinical staff who would otherwise have searched and reviewed the literature themselves, there is a requirement for individuals and teams to make space in their busy work week to participate in EPGs and/or review the CEBIS evidence summary and relevant full-text articles. The CEBIS model requires the evidence be examined in some detail so it can be applied to the local situation. All CEBIS specialists have had EPGs and other meetings postponed or cancelled because of other demands on clinicians' time or have created evidence summaries that may never have been read or given the attention required. Apart from frustration caused for individuals, this means the evidence is not getting into practice as quickly as it should. Ways in which the CEBIS team try to counter this include being a regular presence in clinical departments, reminding individuals about work done for them, e.g., handing over printouts of papers and summaries or doing a quick review during another meeting, and being as flexible as possible around timing and location of meetings. Tailoring the evidence summary or presentation to users' preferences can also save time. Until the importance of interprofessional collaboration for evidence-based decision making and learning is recognized and time made available for its application by managers at the hospital and by policy makers nationally, health service staff will continue to struggle with this issue.

Earning the Respect of Clinical Staff

CEBIS specialists and other information professionals can often face hostilities and a lack of willingness to include information professionals within clinical teams. It has been wrongly presumed in the past that CEBIS specialists do not belong or cannot contribute anything of use to clinical teams. Their presence at clinical meetings may be questioned or prevented. This can be, and has been overcome in some cases by persistence on the part of the information professional and by providing a working example of how involvement can help to improve a clinical team or situation to a skeptical individual or group. Another option is to build a reputation via a supportive individual within a specialty with the hope of development into more team-based collaboration at a later date. The CEBIS team has limited capacity, so initially targeting people or teams who are willing and able to collaborate is a more efficient use of time than pursuing reluctant users!

While it is important to promote the information specialist's skill set and value in evidence-based health care, the CEBIS team have also found acknowledging their own limitations in terms of clinical expertise and patient knowledge is crucial in earning the respect of clinical colleagues. For example, if a CEBIS specialist receives an unclear referral, the requestor can be asked for further explanation or background information, to ensure the most relevant and useful response possible is received. The "scoping search" is a tool sometimes used by CEBIS specialists to support this questioning and clarification process. The list of abstracts or references arising from a quick search of a single database, usually PubMed, is sent to the user, who is asked to select information best meeting their needs, to inform further searching and the creation of an evidence summary. Service users and CEBIS specialists work together on teasing out the real meaning and purpose of the question at hand. The majority of clinicians appreciate this approach far more than if the CEBIS specialist tried to figure out what was required and sent useless references and papers in response. Persistence may be needed to get the necessary background information or clarification from a clinician, but time put in by both parties at this stage will save time later. Promoting all three components of evidence-based health care (evidence, clinical expertise, and patient) and approaching this collaborative process with humility, openness, and a willingness to learn has helped CEBIS specialists earn the respect of many clinical staff.

SUCCESSES

Specialist Knowledge and Skills

None of the CEBIS specialists have an educational background or practical experience in medicine or any allied health profession. Working closely with clinical teams and running many searches in specialty areas can involve a steep learning curve. Inevitably, the CEBIS specialist develops knowledge of specific subject areas, as well as an awareness of topics of particular concern or interest to the staff they work with. This is a rewarding process, enabling the information specialist to do his or her job more quickly and effectively.

CEBIS specialists have built strong working relationships with clinicians and gained a clearer understanding of the local patient population. This is particularly true of the specialty teams with which they work most closely as exemplified in the case studies above. However, there are also individuals across the hospital who are regular users of the service for specific purposes.

Another skill that CEBIS specialists have developed is making connections between clinicians and other contacts either within or external to the hospital, therefore extending collaboration and communication beyond the CEBIS—clinician axis. For example, the library is located alongside teams managing the content of the hospital's document management system in the organizational structure of the hospital. Familiarity with these teams and how they work can be of benefit to clinical staff developing guidelines or patient information leaflets, as described in the Ophthalmology case study earlier in the chapter.

Working on different referrals from across the hospital, and having previous work stored on the IT system, enables CEBIS specialists to notice when different people are working on similar topics or projects. There have been occasions when CEBIS has enabled individuals or teams to connect and share knowledge. Acting in this mediator/broker role is beneficial to CEBIS users and enhances the reputation of the CEBIS team as knowledgeable, helpful, and timesaving collaborators.

Duplication in research was identified as a concern when CEBIS was approached several times with a "new" research idea that had been carried out previously, nationally, internationally, or even at University Hospital itself. A closer collaborative working relationship with the hospital's Research and Development (R&D) team has raised awareness about similar past projects or ones currently being undertaken, including which subjects have been investigated previously, but have failed to progress and why, therefore removing the element of repeatedly unsuccessful research projects.

CEBIS and National Policy

Health Education England (HEE) has identified embedded roles, where information professionals proactively collaborate with teams in their place of work, as an effective model which should be expanded across the NHS:

> *Librarians comprise a small, specialised workforce in the NHS. [...] Increasingly, they are called upon to take a more active role as knowledge brokers. Health Education England recognises the value of these enhanced roles in which librarians share their expertise with teams in the workplace, enabling staff to find, evaluate and use evidence.*[8]

CEBIS has been recognized as an example of this model in HEE's development framework:

> *The work of the University Hospitals Coventry and Warwickshire NHS Trust's CEBIS (Clinical Evidence Based Information System) exemplifies the beneficial impact of proactive customer focused knowledge services on therapeutic decisions and patient outcomes, patient experience and safety and cost savings.*[9]

Publications and Conference Presentations

CEBIS specialists have delivered well-received presentations at conferences in the United Kingdom and overseas, including the Medical Library Association (MLA) 2013 annual meeting in Boston[10]; Health Libraries Group (HLG) 2014 in Oxford, United Kingdom; European Association of Health Information and Libraries (EAHIL) 2016 in Seville, Spain[11]; and Evidence Live 2016 in Oxford, United Kingdom.[12] The latter was an attempt to spread the word to clinicians and other evidence-based healthcare experts about the value of collaborating with information specialists. During a show of hands vote requested by the chair at the end of the presentation, all but one of the audience members stated that they felt having a service such as CEBIS available at their organization would be of use and benefit to them.

CEBIS also regularly contributes to clinical publications or poster presentations. Recent publications and posters authored by clinicians who acknowledge collaboration with CEBIS include a systematic review relating to the UK's 2-week wait referral system in oncology[13] and a poster at the Royal College of Paediatric and Child Health Conference held in April 2015 in Birmingham, United Kingdom.[14]

COLLECTING EXAMPLES OF IMPACT

An electronic outcomes survey is sent to the requestor after the completion of each CEBIS referral. The CEBIS specialists recently remodeled the outcomes survey, basing it on a survey designed by Brettle et al.[15] It contains 11 questions targeted at meeting the values and objectives held by HEE as well as local organizational objectives, mission, and values. This should enable advocacy at hospital level and demonstrate impact aligned with organizational and national strategy. The purpose of requesting feedback is to evaluate the effectiveness of the service and make any necessary improvements, while encouraging clinicians to reflect on how CEBIS may have helped or could help in the future, as well as measuring and demonstrating the impact and value of both CEBIS and of information professionals embedded in clinical teams.

Unfortunately, the survey response rate has been low, and feedback is often delivered verbally in passing, or by brief email, rather than in a more effective survey format allowing for proper recording of impact. It can be more productive to sit with clinicians in person for a short period of time to go through the survey and record their answers; however, it has been noted this may not encourage honesty if clinicians have anything negative to say. The aim is to create a mixed-methods approach requesting feedback with gentle encouragement to use the online survey and with CEBIS specialists taking better note of any mentioned outcomes arising during conversations with clinicians. A recent development is the recording and publishing of "case studies," using feedback taken from the survey responses, and asking clinicians for a short interview where all necessary information is recorded and translated into a case study format to publish nationally, and in some cases internationally. Fig. 1.3 illustrates the impact and benefit of CEBIS from the perspective and experience of clinicians, via a selection of responses to the online survey.

DEMAND FOR AND INVESTMENT IN THE SERVICE

The continued funding of three CEBIS specialist posts can be seen as a marker of the service's success in delivering value and impact, especially in a time when NHS hospitals are under financial strain. The success of CEBIS

How did CEBIS change patient care as a result of the information given on this occasion?

- "Referral, Patient choice of treatment, Advice given to patient or family"
- "Advice given to patient or family"

What adverse events did using CEBIS aviod on this occasion?

- "Patient mortality, Patient morbidity"
- "Prevented repetition of research"

How would you sum up the impact of the service provided on this occasion?

- "Information has provided evidence comparing two treatment options. Will disseminate to other staff safe in the knowledge that current evidence dictates it to be true."
- "Helped save time by providing the papers required for a publication, which will helped in writing a funding bid for a project."
- "Very helpful to save time in terms of literature search myself and educate two specialist teams with up to date best evidence"
- "Excellent service which provides help and support in challenging situations. Extremely valuable."

Are there any other comments you would like to add?

- "This is a good example of how the expertise of knowledge specialists can support clinicians and academics in research to help improve patient outcomes."
- "Using CEBIS on this occasion helped to do a systematic review on topic for grant application. Study opened at UHCW in Pre-Pilot which will be carried forward to full trial at a later date once funding has been obtained."
- "Very helpful, some studies were not directly relevant to the question but helped me to understand the issue as a whole. I appreciate the data is very limited on this subject and this is evident with the ongoing HIP trial which is yet to publish data (which was included in the search). Overall very useful and efficient and crucial in topics such as this which are difficult to find data on."

Figure 1.3 A selection of online survey responses.

as the library's flagship service is also used to support other business cases or funding requests, such as the purchase of electronic full-text archives of many journals previously held in print format and removed because of alternative use of the space.

There is demand for embedded CEBIS specialists in additional clinical teams, as well as in corporate departments. Present capacity does not allow this, so expansion of the service is a future aim. More understanding at a hospital corporate level is the most likely source of financial backing to enable expansion in terms of staffing, and this is a key goal. Proving benefit and impact in-house is therefore essential, though positive outcomes for patients and clinicians tend to hold more weight in a clinical setting rather than in a boardroom, where chief concerns are often financial. There is also anecdotal evidence of demand for a CEBIS-type service regionally, as clinical staff, particularly trainee doctors, often rotate to other hospitals. If they have been regular CEBIS users, they bemoan the lack of such a service elsewhere. National strategy recommending "clinical and outreach models are expanded to become standard practice"[16] supports the expansion of services similar to CEBIS, and is a major implication for the future of all health sciences libraries and knowledge services across England. For these reasons, more of this kind of collaboration between clinical staff and information professionals needs to happen in the future.

CONCLUSION

Strategic collaboration has been a key factor in the evolution of the role of the CL and has played an essential role in the creation and development of CEBIS. From embedding the specialist role within clinical teams, to bidding for investment to develop an IT system, without strategic collaboration between managers, clinicians, and information professionals, CEBIS would not exist. Interprofessional collaboration has been welcomed in some areas, misunderstood in others, and openly rejected in the minority. However, with adaptability and resilience, information professionals can overcome many of the barriers associated with working in multidisciplinary settings and have a demonstrable positive impact on patient care outcomes.

Through collaborative working between Information Professionals and clinicians, awareness has been raised of the importance of library skills and resources at a corporate level. The reputation of the library at a regional level has been enhanced through working closely with clinicians who recognize the impact of the service and bemoan the lack of this support when moving on to other hospitals.

REFERENCES

1. Sackett DL, Rosenberg WMC, Gray JAM, Haynes RB, Richardson WS. Evidence-based medicine: what it is and what it isn't. *BMJ*. 1996;312(7023):71—72. https://www.ncbi.nlm.nih.gov/pmc/articles/PMC2349778/.
2. University Hospitals Coventry and Warwickshire NHS Trust. *2016 — 2017 Annual Report: University Hospitals Coventry and Warwickshire NHS Trust*; May 25, 2017. https://www.uhcw.nhs.uk/clientfiles/File/Annual%20Reports%20and%20Quality%20Accounts/2016-17%20Annual%20Report.pdf.
3. Makhzoum O, Elaraoud I, Andreatta W, Hero M. Poster: the role of oral linezolid in the management of postoperative endophthalmitis. In: *17th Euretina Congress, 7—10 September 2017. Barcelona, Spain*; September 2017. http://www.euretina.org/barcelona2017/programme/posters-details.asp?id=14297.

4. Barry P, Cordoves L, Gardner S. *ESCRS Guidelines for Prevention and Treatment of Endophthalmitis Following Cataract Surgery: Data, Dilemmas and Conclusions*. Temple House, Temple Road, Blackrock, Co Dublin, Ireland: The European Society of Cataract and Refractive Surgeons; 2013. http://www.escrs.org/downloads/Endophthalmitis-Guidelines.pdf.
5. Kim CH, Chen MF, Coleman AL. Adjunctive steroid therapy versus antibiotics alone for acute endophthalmitis after intraocular procedure. *Cochrane Database Syst Rev*. February 22, 2017;(2):CD012131. https://doi.org/10.1002/14651858.CD012131.
6. [Blog]. *Does the NHS Need More Money? Kings Fund*; November 20, 2017. https://www.kingsfund.org.uk/publications/articles/does-nhs-need-more-money.
7. Triggle N. *10 Charts that Show Why the NHS Is in Trouble* [website]. BBC News; January 05, 2018. http://www.bbc.co.uk/news/health-42572110.
8. Lacey Bryant S. *NHS Library and Knowledge Services in England: Policy. Knowledge for Healthcare Policy Statement Annex A*. NHS Health Education England; October 31 , 2016. https://hee.nhs.uk/sites/default/files/documents/Knowledge%20for%20Healthcare%20-Policy%20Statement%20Nov%202016.pdf.
9. Edwards C, Ferguson L. *Knowledge for Healthcare: Quality and Impact. CILIP Update*; November 2015. https://www.hee.nhs.uk/sites/default/files/documents/Knowledge%20for%20Healthcare%20-%20Quality%20and%20Impact.pdf.
10. Conway A, LeMay J. A system for interdependency: a quality improvement study. In: *One Health: Information in an Interdependent World: MLA ICML ICAHIS ICLC, 3–8 May 2013. Boston, MA, USA*; May 2013. http://www.mlanet.org/d/do/1922.
11. Brown A, Dunlop A. CEBIS: bringing research knowledge to the clinician and patient to inform evidence based practice. In: *EAHIL 2016, 6–11 June 2016. Seville, Spain*; June 2016. http://www.bvsspa.es/eahil2016/b5/.
12. Brown A, Dunlop A. CEBIS: bringing research knowledge to the clinician and patient to inform evidence based practice. In: *Evidence Live 2016, June; 22-24. Oxford, UK*; June 22, 2016. http://evidencelive.org/wp-content/uploads/2016/06/CEBIS-Evidence-Live.pdf.
13. Mozdiak E, Tsertsvadze A, McFarlane M, et al. The effect of the 2-week wait referral system on the detection of and mortality from colorectal cancer: protocol of a systematic review and meta-analysis. *Syst Rev*. October 2016 26;5(1):182. https://www.ncbi.nlm.nih.gov/pmc/articles/PMC5081696/pdf/13643_2016_Article_358.pdf.
14. Roe L, Neuling K, Coad N, Dunlop A. Poster: hypoglycaemia secondary to 6 mercaptopurine in leukaemia treatment. In: *RCPCH Annual Conference, 28–30 April 2015. Birmingham, UK*. 2015.
15. Brettle A, Maden-Jenkins M, Anderson L, et al. Evaluating clinical librarian services: a systematic review. *HILJ*. 2011;28(1):3–22. https://doi.org/10.1111/j.1471-1842.2010.00925.
16. Health Education England. *Knowledge for Healthcare: A Development Framework for NHS Library and Knowledge Services in England, 2014*. NHS Health Education England; January 27, 2015. https://hee.nhs.uk/sites/default/files/documents/Knowledge%20for%20healthcare%20-%20a%20development%20framework.pdf.

CHAPTER 2

Collaboration is Key: Advancing the Academic Health Sciences Library's Mission Through Campus Partnerships Within Library Spaces

Janice M. Jaguszewski, Lisa A. McGuire
Health Sciences Libraries, University of Minnesota, Minneapolis, MN, United States

INTRODUCTION

From 2014 to 2017, the University of Minnesota's Bio-Medical Library and the Wangensteen Historical Library of Biology and Medicine (collectively referred to as the Health Sciences Libraries, HSL) positioned themselves as a vital component of a brand new interprofessional Health Sciences Education Center (HSEC). Design and development were completed in 2017, culminating in funding by the Minnesota legislature, with construction scheduled for completion in early 2020. The vision behind HSEC is to develop and deliver an interprofessional curriculum and active learning environment for five of the six schools of the Academic Health Center (AHC—Nursing, Medicine, Dentistry, Public Health, Pharmacy; Veterinary Medicine has its own branch library on the St. Paul campus 5 miles away). HSEC brings together active learning classrooms, student support services, library expertise and technologies, and an extensive simulation center all in one building. To contribute to this vision, an HSL planning team developed a partnership model with units from across the AHC, and the larger campus, leveraging a wide range of expertise and building a new and highly robust infrastructure where all partners benefit and the HSL mission is advanced.

HSL entitled the model, "Space as a Service to Advance Learning, Research and Professional Practice" and articulated the following overarching vision:

The Health Sciences Libraries are a...

Strategic Collaborations in Health Sciences Libraries
ISBN 978-0-08-102258-0
https://doi.org/10.1016/B978-0-08-102258-0.00002-1
Copyright © 2019 Jean P. Shipman and M.J. Tooey. Published by Elsevier Limited. All rights reserved.

- **Common good**, where exceptional staff with deep expertise facilitate the knowledge lifecycle and solve information problems
- **Connector**, strategically linking people, resources, services, information, and technology to achieve common goals
- **Creative catalyst**, prompting new insights into learning/research and offering new models for shared spaces
- **Service-rich environment** available to all

The model itself centers on (1) identifying user needs, (2) developing collaborations and partnerships leveraging and optimizing resources, and (3) jointly creating space-enabled services to meet user needs. For example, in order to enhance learning (user need), HSL, instructional designers, the Center for Educational Innovation (University-wide support for faculty development), and academic technologists (collaborators) will enable instructors to explore and integrate new technologies into their teaching through an educational technology sandbox (space-enabled service).[1] See Table 3.1 for more examples.

HSL is using the three years of design and development to prototype a number of new space-enabled services and approach the development of potential partners in a methodical and strategic way. As a result, HSL is able to demonstrate its expertise and leadership role to the AHC, identify successful approaches for future investment, learn from failures on a small scale, and cultivate partners with a commitment to long-term success before the building is completed.

This chapter offers strategies for success when cultivating and working with partners, using the HSL partnership model and resulting new suite of space-enabled services (e.g., Faculty Commons, Virtual and Augmented Reality Studio, 1:Button Studio, Visualization Lab, Wangensteen Historical Library, and Innovation Space). It also discusses impact and lessons learned.

LITERATURE REVIEW

Academic health sciences libraries are actively engaged with their health professions faculty to partner in advancing teaching, learning, and research. The business literature abounds with varying definitions of partnership and collaboration, and the terms are used interchangeably. Wood and Gray state "collaboration occurs when a group of autonomous stakeholders of a problem engage in an interactive process, using shared rules, norms, and structures, to act or decide on issues related to that domain."[2] Mohr and Spekman define partnership as "purposive strategic relationships between

Table 3.1 Examples from the "Space as a Service" Model at the University of Minnesota Health Sciences Libraries

Learning need	Collaborators	Space-enabled service
Faculty skill development in teaching with technology	Instructional designers; Academic Technology Services; Center for Educational Innovation	Faculty commons with an educational technology sandbox
Professional skills development in simulated environments	Simulation Center; curriculum development; researchers	Virtual and augmented reality lab
Digital content creation and multimedia production	Office of Information Technology; instructional designers; instructors	1:Button video recording studio and specialized software to support
Data analysis and visual representation of data	Data visualization specialists; geographic information system specialists	Technology-rich data visualization environment
Historical context of each profession	Instructors; development officers; student organizations	Specialized Library devoted to the integration of rare books, manuscripts, and artifacts into curricula
Problem-based learning and entrepreneurship	Medical Device Center; Innovation Fellows program; Information Systems office	Innovation space that provides makerspace technologies and intentional programming

independent firms who share compatible goals, strive for mutual benefit, and acknowledge a high level of mutual interdependence."[3] For the purposes of this chapter, collaboration is defined as a shared approach to addressing a specific, well-defined user need; and partnership refers to a more formalized, long-term process of ongoing engagement. Essentially, partnerships provide an overarching program realized through numerous collaborative efforts.

Over the past 30 years, the health sciences library literature offers many case studies describing a wide range of collaborative activities and/or partnerships. Examples include academic health science libraries joining with public libraries to form cooperative networks providing consumer health information,[4] consortia agreements among Big Ten institutions providing online guides to health topics in the early days of the Internet,[5] partnerships with community health nursing students increasing access to Spanish-language consumer health materials in public health clinics,[6] development of intensive support for researchers with the informationist model,[7] library support for medical schools with Clinical and Translational Science Awards,[8] collaboration with a university's office of research supporting compliance with National Institutes of Health funding requirements,[9] partnering with faculty showing increased reproducibility of systematic review searching,[10] and the enrichment of collaborations between health science libraries and IT departments.[11]

Comprehensive models of strategic collaboration and partnership applied systematically to new situations are harder to find in the library literature, although components of models are described. For example, Allee et al. outline the proactive planning of the Taubman Library at the University of Michigan which was undertook to remain relevant to its affiliates. Their process included redefining the library mission as a partner and collaborator to their health profession schools, eliminating "traditional" library work and tasks, redefining librarian roles as liaisons, forming teams to respond to new campus initiatives, and renovating space to respond to changing curricula, including self-directed learning.[12] New library directors at Northwestern and Weill Cornell Medical College did not have the luxury of time to develop a partnership model, but instead were charged with rapidly creating a compelling plan to meet their institutions' future information needs. Both libraries utilized Kotter's approach to change management—one element of a successful model—to implement new services, build staff buy-in, communicate effectively, and motivate staff to engage in a continuous improvement process.[13]

The HSL "Space as a Service" model described in the introduction and in the article by Jaguszewski and McGuire offers a model of collaboration.[14] This model may be extended by systematically applying the seven strategies described in this chapter to turn collaborations into stronger, more formalized, and long-lasting partnerships.

SEVEN STRATEGIES FOR SUCCESSFUL PARTNERSHIPS IN THE BIO-MEDICAL AND WANGENSTEEN LIBRARIES

HSL intentionally designed the library spaces in the new HSEC to facilitate the knowledge lifecycle: discovery, use, creation, and sharing. A conceptual framework for each space was developed and included the involvement of strategic collaborators who could become formal partners. Throughout this design process, HSL utilized seven strategies to ensure the partnerships being developed, and on which HSL would rely, would be successful. Each strategy is addressed here in the context of one or more of HSL's spaces.

Strategy 1. Shared Overarching Goals and Mutual Benefit: the Faculty Commons

Every potential partnership should begin with the articulation of shared overarching goals, accounting for the mission of each partner. Conversations and planning must reveal each partner's underlying assumptions to ensure everyone is in alignment. What is the library trying to accomplish? Who are the stakeholders? What are the partners' goals? What should students and faculty be able to do as a result of their interaction with the services provided in each space? What does each partner bring to support these services, and how does each advance its mission and benefit from the partnership? These questions need to be explored in depth to establish a strong foundation on which to build the partnership.

As an example, in HSEC, a Faculty Commons will offer a technology-rich space with an adjacent customizable video recording studio supporting the teaching needs of faculty, enabling them to test new pedagogical techniques and develop new ways to integrate technology and digital content into their teaching with support from peers, instructional designers, academic technologists, the Center for Educational Innovation, the AHC Interprofessional Education Leaders Forum, and librarians. HSL invited a range of potential partners to numerous planning meetings to discuss and deeply explore key foundational questions. Early in the process, the following shared goals were identified:

- Faculty will design and create high-quality learning environments online and in person by
  - learning about new tools, techniques, and technologies
  - developing new online content, e.g., open textbooks, streaming video, and virtual reality software
  - identifying licensed content and open educational resources
  - optimizing the features of the learning management system
  - integrating all of these resources into curricula with strategic interprofessional components.
- Faculty will explore and apply research-based pedagogies.
- Faculty will understand and apply a range of formative and summative methods of assessment.
- Faculty will increase their awareness of and make connections with relevant experts throughout the University (e.g., Center for Educational

Innovation, AHC academic technologists and instructional designers, Simulation Center, and library specialists).

These goals will guide the selection of new educational technologies, facilitate connections between instructors and campus experts, and inform the development of workshops, consulting services, and a formal professional development series.

Strategy 2. Compatible Cultures: Virtual and Augmented Reality Studio

HSL sought partners who share the values of its organizational culture: recognizing co-location is not collaboration, embracing collaboration over competition, understanding leveraging resources involves both give and take, listening to others, welcoming constructive feedback, and working through difficulties to achieve common goals. For example, a Virtual and Augmented Reality Studio (VR/AR) will provide an immersive learning and research environment supporting the creation and use of virtual and augmented reality, enabling students and faculty to experience the world from another person's perspective and learn new skills in a realistic, virtual environment (e.g., a simulated operating room, or a country experiencing a natural disaster). The Simulation Center has been a significant partner in the development of technologies and programming for this studio, bringing a spirit of collaboration and generosity to the table. It offers vision and possibility and can think laterally and strategically, e.g., suggesting ways in which to integrate 3D resources HSL licenses into VR simulations to create new experiences. It is also flexible and user-focused, ensuring the needs of students and faculty guide its curricula. As a result, it actively supports HSL and its mission, suggesting new ways in which to share expertise to staff spaces and provide consulting services. It is focused on the big picture and offers a sense of confidence and openness, and a clarity of purpose, avoiding issues of territoriality and values result over recognition. Because of these compatible cultures and ways of working, HSL and the Simulation Center have been able to develop completely new ideas about how VR and AR may be integrated into an interprofessional curriculum.

Strategy 3. Clear Roles and Responsibilities: 1:Button Studio

Successful partnerships require each contributor's roles and responsibilities be clearly defined. HSL must articulate the goals it is striving to accomplish and what specific knowledge, skills, and resources it brings to the partnership. Where and when does HSL lead, and where and when does it follow? What are its specific areas of primacy, and is an understanding of this primacy shared among the partners? Would a formal memorandum of understanding between partners, including clear roles and responsibilities, be useful, particularly when partners have no direct authority over one another?

One very successful prototype implemented in the Bio-Medical Library, and which informed spaces and services in HSEC, was the 1:Button Studio concept. This space offers an easy-to-use high-definition video recording studio, including professional lighting, and is based on a service originally developed by Penn State University Libraries.[15] This partnership was originally developed between the University Libraries and the Office of Information Technology (OIT). OIT's clear role was focused on the mechanics of the studio—implementing, maintaining, and refreshing the hardware, software, lighting, sound-proofing, and physical space for an optimal audio- and video recording experience. They recognized that the Bio-Medical Library's location in the heart of the AHC provided many service benefits, such as expansive hours of operation, unmediated access for users, and on-site assistance, especially during evenings and weekends. The service model was then expanded to leverage the liaisons' relationships with faculty and instructional designers in each school and college to integrate the creation of video content into the curricula. Faculty began to understand how recordings could be applied to flip their classrooms, to see the possibilities of integrated online content (e.g., streaming video, images, and data; licensed, purchased, and freely available), and to work with liaisons and instructional designers to create student assignments involving multimedia projects.

With this expanded programmatic approach in which a service model is layered on top of the provision of equipment and spaces, OIT's role as service owner was thoughtfully transferred to the Bio-Medical Library, and then to the University Libraries as a whole when new studios were added to two other campus libraries. The University Libraries developed standardized branding, marketing, and promotion techniques; implemented an online reservation system; established policies and procedures; and developed methods for evaluation. They also worked closely with instructional designers to ensure faculty were following recommended practices and coordinated conversations when their expertise was needed. By recognizing when roles were changing and expanding, and talking through these issues as they arose, the Bio-Medical Library and OIT created a seamless and highly supportive service for both faculty and students that will be expanded to three studios in the HSEC, plus one customizable studio as part of the Faculty Commons technology sandbox.

Strategy 4. Dedicated Staffing: Visualization Lab

Partnerships, from their beginning, require a significant amount of time, attention, and care. As a result, dedicated staffing is needed. In the Bio-Medical Library, the clinical information librarian had an interest in and aptitude for visualization concepts and technologies and was given the opportunity to research the possibilities and develop a prototype for a data visualization center. He immersed himself in learning software, understanding best practices, networking with experts on campus, selecting hardware and software, promoting the space, helping library assistants develop baseline skills to get people started, and outlining workshops and courses. As planning for HSEC proceeded and many new technologies and spaces were identified, it became clear that a new full-time position was needed to provide strategic leadership both for the planning process and for the working partnerships from across campus. As a result, a vacant position, previously focused on informatics, was reconceived as an emerging technology and innovation strategist, and the clinical information librarian moved into this position (the clinical responsibilities were then replaced by a new hire). The clinical information librarian brought both subject matter expertise and strong interpersonal skills to the job. There are now plans to build on the data visualization center to plan for a Visualization Lab in HSEC offering a collaborative teaching and learning space with large displays for data visualization exploration, facilitating the analysis of complex data, and providing professional students with the skills to more effectively communicate information to patients through visual and graphical formats. This librarian is identifying the advanced technical expertise needed for a core curriculum and programming and is developing partnerships with Design, Computer Science and Computer Engineering, Epidemiology, and Health Informatics, among others, to ensure the services are designed in time for the HSEC's opening.

Strategy 5. Trust and Respect: Wangensteen Historical Library

The Owen H. Wangensteen Historical Library of Biology and Medicine (WHL) is a preeminent collection of 80,000 rare books, manuscripts, and artifacts from the 15th to the early 20th century. Each year WHL supports 500 on-site scholars from around the world, is integrated into 60 courses

(1500 students) contextualizing the history of the health professions, and hosts numerous outreach events. The curator has achieved incredible success despite the fact the WHL is currently hidden on the fifth floor of the Bio-Medical Library's building, and outside of the Bio-Medical Library's perimeter, requiring access through a separate elevator. As a result, the curator works tirelessly to promote the collection, develop faculty partnerships, and build awareness of the WHL's services and staff expertise.

A goal from the very beginning of planning for HSEC was to increase the visibility of WHL in the new building. HSL was one of six core planning teams, the others being classroom management, academic technology, student services, interprofessional education, and the simulation center. Most of these planning teams were completely unaware of the stature of the WHL collection and its use by faculty, students, and scholars. As a result, over the course of the design process, the HSL planning team clearly and repeatedly described the level of engagement WHL curators have with faculty across the disciplines, with community partners who collaborate on outreach activities, and with scholars from around the world conducting research. The HSL space team invited other team leads out for coffee and conversation, the curators offered tours and passionate presentations to architects and administrators, and the WHL director described the centrality and value of the collection itself, much of which is irreplaceable, to the capital planning and facilities management team. In turn, the HSL planning team listened to the other team leads and actively worked to understand their priorities and visibly support them during budget discussions. This sustained effort at building relationships resulted in a deep sense of mutual trust and respect critical to any collaboration or partnership. The process was not always smooth, and there were plenty of disagreements, but in the end, the effort devoted to developing a solid foundation of trust paid off.

WHL will be located in a much more visible location within HSEC, on a busy concourse teaming with students and faculty moving to and from active learning classrooms, and patients making their way to clinics and the teaching hospital. With glass-front walls facing the concourse, themed exhibits displaying elements of the collection will invite passersby into the space to learn more about the collection. WHL will have its own classroom, which will also be visible to those on the concourse, as will the reading room used by scholars working with the collection, highlighting the research and teaching activities within the spaces. None of this would have been possible, or supported, if trusting and respectful relationships had not been cultivated throughout the planning process.

Strategy 6. Ability to Navigate Relationships and Politics: Maker/Innovation Space

HSL recognized that innovation and entrepreneurship are becoming important elements in the education of health professions students, and students and faculty would need spaces in which to experiment, create, and innovate solutions to health-care problems. A Maker/Innovation Space within HSEC will facilitate experiential learning and encourage creativity and collaboration through design development, rapid prototyping, and exposure to emerging technologies in health care. As a result, students will develop an understanding of entrepreneurship and the potential for commercialization.

As a number of campus colleges (e.g., Design, Science and Engineering) and units (e.g., Earl E. Bakken Medical Devices Center—BMDC) have already developed these types of spaces on campus, HSL was aware of the importance of articulating why a space in HSEC is needed and to navigate the politics around campus space issues and the "ownership" of related activities in other areas. For example, early conversations between the HSL planning team and the staff at BMDC quickly revealed that the BMDC needed additional space and saw expansion into HSEC as a way to secure it. HSL, on the other hand, was seeking a programmatic partner with shared goals. Through several discussions, it was determined the two entities did not have enough in common to develop a full partnership, but clarified how they could support one another's separate goals and missions. The Maker/Innovation Space in HSEC will serve as an early introduction for students to explore prototyping and entrepreneurship, and the BMDC will continue to focus on the advanced needs of researchers who require access to high-end equipment and are ready to commercialize their medical technologies. Staff in the Maker/Innovation Space will make referrals to BMDC as appropriate and help raise the profile of its services. BMDC, in turn, will be available for consulting and advising. Although there are many other potential partners for the Maker/Innovation Space, HSL recognized that sometimes the purpose and mission of another unit are just too different to form a true partnership. Co-location, without shared goals leveraging the skills of each group to create something new, is not an actual partnership. As a result, HSL preserved the original intent of the Maker/Innovation Space in HSEC, maintained positive relations with BMDC, and preserved its social capital with the AHC.

Strategy 7. Communication, Communication, Communication

Developing and communicating a vision for the future, up, down, and across an organization, is critical. All partners must develop a continuous communication loop with their own internal staff, with one another, and with external stakeholders.

Change management, as noted in the Literature Review section, is an important component of partnership models. Within HSL, the planning team communicates regularly to staff about progress on the predesign and design processes. Updates are included in a biweekly newsletter, presentations and opportunities for feedback take place at monthly all-staff meetings, and one-on-one conversations happen regularly between individuals, their supervisors and the HSL director. HSL staff need to understand why new partnerships are important, where they fit in the partnership model, why new positions dedicated to working with partners will be developed, and how their own responsibilities may change.

Partners must be in constant and open communication with one another. They need to understand when to consult more broadly, how to approach administration, when one partner should represent the others (because they have earned trust and respect!), and when to speak with a united voice. The HSL planning team kept a variety of handouts with clear talking points and impactful images to share at meetings when key programmatic points needed to be reinforced. HSL is now working with its partners to develop shared communication vehicles reflecting a comprehensive vision for spaces and services throughout the HSEC.

Communication with external stakeholders becomes increasingly important as the details of a partnership solidify and take shape in order to gain visibility and wider support for new initiatives. Messaging is most effective when delivered in a variety of formats (e.g., print, online, video, social media, and in person) and repeated with regularity. Communicating early and often is essential. A good indicator that a message is finally reaching an audience is recognizing when a message feels like it has run its course and just cannot be repeated one more time. It is likely this is the exact point at which an audience is just beginning to listen and appreciate what is being said.

One tricky area to keep in mind is branding. As partners work closely together in an integrated service model, the brand for the service becomes extremely important. As a result, each partner's individual contributions can become lost. How important is it to maintain a separate identity within the partnership? Can a balance be struck? Can a logo or tagline reflect the parts that make an effective whole?

Robust communication plans that address target audiences, demonstrate benefits including inclusivity, develop support and champions, and brand services to develop recognition are a critical part of a successful partnership.

IMPACT AND CONCLUSION

The partnerships developed by prototyping new spaces and services in the years leading up to a new building, and the deep relationships developed in designing the building itself, resulted in numerous benefits with significant impact. Specifically, HSL and its partners were able to:

- Gather a range of perspectives and gain a deeper understanding of possibilities
- Create something completely new and position everyone involved to realize an ambitious new vision
- Leverage resources (e.g., space, equipment, funding, and promotion/marketing)
- Increase staffing capacity and define the specialized expertise needed to reside in HSL and within the partners
- Share risk and encourage each partner to try out new ideas
- Gain support through a united voice, with champions to reinforce messaging and strengthen influence

Ultimately, HSL was able to effectively advocate for a re-envisioned library within HSEC by developing relationships, building champions, and establishing shared goals in advance throughout the 3-year predesign and design planning process. Its many spaces and services all have well-defined goals, descriptive narratives, clearly articulated benefits to students and faculty, carefully outfitted furnishings and technologies, and partners who are equally committed to realizing the vision and contributing to its success.

The HSL planning team also developed new skill sets that may continue to be refined, increasing the team's effectiveness. Team members learned how to navigate organizational politics; utilize pilot programs effectively; cultivate champions; develop the ability to influence and persuade with a particular emphasis on benefit to the student, the faculty member, the AHC's reputation, and donor relations; publicly recognize, thank, and celebrate partners; recognize when to compromise; and anticipate and mitigate risks.

While HSEC is under construction, HSL will work with its existing partners, and cultivate new ones to further develop programming and curricular integration. It is positioned strategically to succeed when HSEC is completed and its doors open.

ACKNOWLEDGMENTS

The authors wish to acknowledge the contributions of our colleagues in HSL in the development of the partnership model and their work to bring a new vision of the Library to life in the future HSEC. Special thanks to the members of the planning team, Lois Hendrickson, Curator of the Wangensteen Historical Library, Jonathan Koffel, Emerging Technology and Innovation Strategist, Emily Reimer, Manager of Access and Information Services, and Liz Weinfurter, School of Nursing Liaison.

REFERENCES

1. Jaguszewski J, McGuire LA. Connector, catalyst and common good: defining the academic library of the 21st century. *LL & M.* February 2018;32(2):1–20.
2. Wood D, Gray B. Toward a comprehensive theory of collaboration. *J Appl Behav Sci.* February 1991;27(2):139–162.
3. Mohr J, Spekman R. Characteristics of partnership success: partnership attributes, communication behavior, and conflict resolution techniques. *Strategic Mgmt J.* February 1994;15(2):135–152.
4. Humphries A, Kochi J. Providing consumer health information through institutional cooperation. *Bull Med Libr Assoc.* January 1994;82(1):52–56.
5. Redman P, Kelly J, Albright E, Anderson P, Mulder C, Schnell E. Common ground: the HealthWeb project as a model for Internet collaboration. *Bull Med Libr Assoc.* October 1997;85(4):325–330.
6. Hitchcock K, Appelt A. Sustainable collaboration for community outreach: lessons from the Spanish Access to Literature/Uso Directo (SALUD) project. *J Med Libr Assoc.* January 2008;96(1):58–60. https://doi.org/10.3163/15365050.96.1.58.
7. Grefsheim S, Whitmore S, Rapp B, Rankin J, Robison R, Canto C. The informationist: building evidence for an emerging health profession. *J Med Lib Assoc.* April 2010;98(2):147–156. https://doi.org/10.3163/1536-5050.98.2.007.
8. Holmes KL, Lyon JA, Johnson LM, Sarli CC, Tennant MR. Library-based clinical and translational research support. *J Med Libr Assoc.* October 2013;101(4):326–335. https://doi.org/10.3163/1536-5050.101.4.017.
9. Black C, Harris B, Mahraj K, Schnitzer AE, Rosenzweig M. Collaboration between the University of Michigan Taubman Health Sciences Library and the University of Michigan Medical School Office of Research. *Med Ref Serv Q.* 2013;32(2):179–184. https://doi.org/10.1080/02763869.2013.776896.
10. Rethlefsen ML, Farrell AM, Osterhaus Trzasko LC, Brigham TJ. Librarian co-authors correlated with higher quality reported search strategies in general internal medicine systematic reviews. *J Clin Epidemiol.* June 2015;68(6):617–626. https://doi.org/10.1016/j./jclinepi.2014.11.025.
11. King S, Cataldi-Roberts E, Wentz E. Meeting at the crossroads: collaboration between information technology departments and health science libraries. *J Med Libr Assoc.* January 2017;105(1):27–33. https://doi.org/10.5195/jmla.2017.104.

12. Allee NJ, Blumenthal J, Jordan K, et al. One institution's experience in transforming the health sciences library of the future. *Med Ref Serv Q*. 2014;33(1):1–16. https://doi.org/10.1080/02763869.2014.866444.
13. Wheeler TR, Holmes KL. Rapid transformation of two libraries using Kotter's Eight Steps of Change. *J Med Libr Assoc*. July 2017;105(3):276–281. https://doi.org/10.5195/jmla.2017.97.
14. Jaguszewski J, McGuire LA. Connector, catalyst and common good: defining the academic library of the 21st century. *LL & M*. February 2018;32(2):1–20.
15. *Penn State University Libraries. One Button Studio*; 2017. Available from: https://libraries.psu.edu/one-button-studio.

CHAPTER 3

Collaborating to Connect the Underserved With Patient Portals

Stephen Kiyoi[1], Courtney Lyles[2], Shobha Sadasivaiah[3]
[1]Library Director, ZSFG Library, UCSF, San Francisco, CA, United States; [2]UCSF Division of General Internal Medicine, Zuckerberg San Francisco General Hospital, San Francisco, CA, United States; [3]UCSF School of Medicine, University of California, San Francisco, CA, United States

INTRODUCTION

This chapter describes a Library-led initiative to engage underserved patients with their health information through a patient portal platform. Patient portals have been rapidly adopted by many health-care systems across the country, but safety-net health-care systems and their patients have often struggled in their implementation, access, and use. This project demonstrates that health sciences libraries and librarians—with their space for teaching and learning, focus on equitable services, direct interactions with patients, expertise in health and digital literacy, and central role within their institutions—are uniquely positioned to lead initiatives to increase engagement with patient portal systems.

THE SETTING

This project takes place in an academically affiliated, urban safety-net health network in the San Francisco Bay Area. The Institute of Medicine defines safety-net institutions as "providers that organize and deliver a significant level of both health care and other health-related services to the uninsured, Medicaid, and other vulnerable populations," and "who by mandate or mission offer access to care regardless of a patient's ability to pay and whose patient population includes a substantial share of uninsured, Medicaid, and other vulnerable patients."[1] The Health Network setting of this project includes a Level 1 Trauma Center Hospital (Hospital) as well as 10 additional community-based primary care clinics (Network). Collectively, these clinics serve over 210,000 low-income adult patients from the city and county, the vast majority of whom are on Medicaid or are uninsured. About 40% of the patient population speaks a primary language other than English (about 15% monolingual Spanish speakers), and approximately 40% have limited health literacy.

Strategic Collaborations in Health Sciences Libraries
ISBN 978-0-08-102258-0
https://doi.org/10.1016/B978-0-08-102258-0.00003-3
Copyright © 2019 Jean P. Shipman and M.J. Tooey. Published by Elsevier Limited. All rights reserved.

The affiliated university provides an on-site library at the Hospital location, staffed by a library director and four full-time equivalent staff responsible for patient engagement, clinical research, hospital archives, and access services. For the remainder of this chapter, "Library" will refer to this on-site Library at the Hospital location and specifically the work of this Library's director and user services coordinator.

THE OPPORTUNITY

Patient Portals Defined

Patient portals are defined by the US Office of the National Coordinator for Health Information Technology, as "a secure online website that gives patients convenient 24-hour access to personal health information from anywhere with an Internet connection."[2] Patient portals are typically provided by an electronic health record vendor and managed by health-care institutions to provide patients with online access to their medical records, including laboratory results, visit summaries, medication lists, and immunization histories. Some patient portals include interactive features, such as the ability for patients to add their own notes and data, exchange secure messages with their providers, schedule routine appointments, and order prescription refills.

The Benefits of Portal Adoption and Use

By connecting patients with their own health information, patient portals have the potential to enhance health knowledge,[3] engage patients with their health,[4] increase personal empowerment,[5] improve transparency and accountability of health-care systems,[6] and ultimately improve health outcomes.[7] Patient portals can also provide an online platform for health-care organizations and their libraries to implement educational interventions at a scale not feasible via in-person interactions. Research has shown many patients have a positive perception of portals' use—approximately 60% of patients using a patient portal find it to be "very useful" and an additional 28% find it to be "somewhat useful."[8] Studies have also shown patient portals can be particularly impactful for patients with chronic illnesses. Active patient portal use in this population has been associated with improved rates of appropriate screening,[9] higher patient satisfaction,[10] and better medication adherence.[11] However, more research is needed to show the impact of patient portals on health-care costs, utilization rates, and long-term health outcomes.[12]

Policy and Business Drivers for Portal Use

The Center for Medicare and Medicaid Services has included patient portals in the larger effort to financially incentivize the adoption of electronic medical records (EMRs) through the Health Information Technology for Economic and Clinical Health (HITECH) Act and the Meaningful Use program.[13] Adoption of EMRs and patient portals have accelerated quickly. Between February 2009, when the HITECH Act was passed into law, and September 2014 alone, Meaningful Use payments had reached more than $25 billion,[14] with as much as $107,750 for each provider who meets all incentive measures.[15] As patient portals become increasingly common and consumer expectations change, health-care systems will be motivated to provide robust patient portal platforms to offer a level of service competitive with other local health-care systems.

THE CHALLENGES

Despite the benefits and opportunities described above, the launch of a patient portal presents unique challenges for urban safety-net systems, serving a linguistically diverse, low-literacy patient population in underresourced settings characterized by high patient to provider ratios, fragmented and underdeveloped health IT infrastructure, and high organizational complexity.

Matthew Effect

Specifically, in safety-net settings, there is a risk that the introduction of a new patient portal platform may inadvertently increase disparities by introducing another hurdle for patients to access aspects of their care. Advantaged patients face fewer obstacles and easily benefit from patient portal use, while underserved patients face more obstacles and may not use portals or benefit from them. This disparity in patient portal access and use may become more consequential as patient portals become an increasingly common and expected channel of patient—provider communication. This dynamic has been described generally by the theory of "The Matthew Effect,"[16] in which new interventions inadvertently yield further advantages for the already advantaged and further disadvantages for underserved patients most needing the new intervention.

Digital Divide

Preliminary research has shown "The Matthew Effect" playing out in practice. Enrollment and usage data from health-care systems like Kaiser have definitively shown patients with higher income, more education, higher levels of health literacy, and patients who are white use existing patient portals more often than those with lower socioeconomic status, and racial/ethnic minority populations. [17-22]

Digital Divide in the Local Setting

An internal, anonymous, unpublished survey of providers and staff in this Network showed the majority reported limited English proficiency, limited literacy, unreliable access to the Internet, unstable housing or homelessness, and cognitive impairment were significant barriers to their patients' use of patient portal systems. Providers and staff also noted their own barriers, including lack of time (84%) and the potential overuse or misuse of messaging by patients (73%). In discussing barriers of particular prominence in the safety-net settings, providers and staff noted that they were already being overburdened. "Providers do more in this system than they do in others."—Anonymous quote. Respondents also noted they provided care for a patient population with a high complexity and burden of health issues as compared with other systems: "Our clients are very sick, homeless, [have] mental issues, drug abuse, [and are] HIV very-complicated clients. Most of the clients I see at [other systems] are not."—Anonymous quote.

THE TEAM

The Library played a significant role in addressing how to effectively engage patients with a patient portal system. Specifically, the Library participated in, and later led the Patient Engagement Workgroup, one of three work groups convened by executive leadership of the Network in late 2013, to begin planning the implementation of a patient portal platform. This work was undertaken under the oversight of a Patient Portal Planning Steering Committee. Along with the other work groups—Technical Support Workgroup and Clinical Content Workgroup—the Patient Engagement Workgroup was responsible for all planning, implementation, and support of patient engagement and patient experience of the portal, including, but not limited to: development of patient education materials, creation of the content of a portal test account for testing and training, integration of enrollment activities into clinical workflows, and calculations of necessary staffing levels. The Patient Engagement Workgroup included a broad cross-section of staff across many disciplines, including physicians, nurses, Information Technology (IT), project managers, management consultants, health educators, librarians, and Library staff. The group also sought input from patients via the Hospital's patient advisory boards, and obtained Institutional Review Board approval for all associated quality improvement and research work.

The Patient Engagement Workgroup convened in November 2013 and met on a biweekly basis over the next year and a half to develop a comprehensive plan to effectively engage patients with the patient portal. The library director received more than 1400 email messages relating to patient portal implementation and support during the initial project period. Over time, as the patient portal was operationalized, a smaller group of the library director, the user services coordinator, a physician champion, and a nursing champion managed the daily work of engaging patients with the portal and coordinating with the vendor regarding user experience issues.

The Library also led the creation of patient education materials for the portal used in both the inpatient and outpatient initiatives described in further detail in the "Inpatient Engagement" and "Outpatient Engagement". These materials were developed with input and approval of the patient advisory boards in two outpatient clinics. Materials included inpatient and outpatient trifolds to be distributed by volunteers and staff to patients, a patient portal tutorial website, and a patient FAQ document. These materials were designed in accordance with the recommendations of the Institute of Medicine Roundtable on Health Literacy.[23] The Patient Engagement Workgroup established a dedicated help line for the portal, initially staffed by Library personnel. The Library also coordinated translation of patient educational materials into local threshold languages—Spanish, Chinese, Vietnamese, Tagalog, and Russian.

INPATIENT ENGAGEMENT

The patient engagement with the portal was organized into separate projects for inpatient (hospital) and outpatient (clinic) enrollment. This section describes the effort to enroll and educate patients in the inpatient setting. Please note the work to develop the patient portal technical requirements and competitively select the patient portal vendor was done by the Patient Portal Planning Steering Committee, before the formation of the Patient Engagement Workgroup, and before the Library's involvement in the project.

Prepilot

The Patient Engagement Workgroup determined a small-scale pilot of the patient registration process was necessary to test standard scripts, assess feasibility of integrating into clinical workflows, determine necessary staffing levels, and identify the primary patient barriers to enrollment. In December 2014, the Patient Engagement Workgroup conducted a small-scale pilot in a single-hospital unit. Work group members, including the library director, approached patients in their rooms to promote the portal and encourage registration. Of the 34 patients discharged during the pilot period, 8 patients created an account, and 26 patients chose not to create one. Reasons for not creating an account included limited English proficiency (11), low computer literacy (5), altered mental status (3), low patient interest (3), IT systems issues (1), issue with proxy workflow (1), and reason not noted (2). As a result of the pilot, the Patient Engagement Workgroup focused on translating the patient education materials and training staff on the use of the patient translation service available through the telephone system in each unit.

Volunteer Program

As a result of the complicated nature of enrollment and high needs of low-literacy patients, the Patient Engagement Workgroup decided to use a volunteer workforce to provide patients with more individualized support. The Library then took on the role of recruiting, training, and coordinating a group of "Volunteer Health Technology Patient Educators," to staff patient engagement efforts. The Library sought consultation from community organizations with experience coordinating volunteer literacy programs, including the Community Technology Network,[24] and the Project Read[25] program in the San Francisco Public Library. The Library then created a "Volunteer Health Technology Patient Educator" job description which was advertised on the Hospital's volunteer page and on volunteermatch.org. Volunteers were screened for their interest in working with underserved patients, experience in customer service or education, and familiarity with online web platforms. Volunteer positions required a minimum of 8 hours a week; 100 hours total. Interest came primarily from local undergraduate students majoring in biology, health communications, and public health. The Library then conducted a 2-hour training for volunteers; including instruction on health communication, patient portals, registration, interpreter services for non-English-speaking patients, and data collection methods. Volunteers were also given a written list of the procedures, covered in the above training, to reference as they visit patients. Finally, members of the Patient Engagement Workgroup shadowed volunteers during the initial provisioning period and continue to conduct weekly group check-ins with volunteers to conduct "Plan Do Study Act"[26] process improvements.

Provisioning Process

In the Hospital setting, the Volunteer Health Technology Patient Educators visit patients in their rooms and invite them to create individual patient portal accounts. If a patient is interested, the volunteer verifies the patient's identity, guides them through the online account creation process, orients them to the portal, and provides personalized computer and health literacy instruction as needed. Volunteers also complete a patient portal data sheet for each patient they approach. This sheet allows the Library to track both operational metrics to assess the volume and impact of the in-person approach, and patient characteristics possibly preventing use of the portal. Patient characteristics are collected anonymously, even if the patient decides not to create a portal account.

Patient TV Integration

As a quality improvement effort, the Library also integrated its educational videos into the inpatient television system. Hospitalized patients can use the television system to view the video and respond to a brief survey to indicate interest in the portal. The goal of this integration is to gather another measure of patient interest in the portal and more specifically target volunteer time toward patients expressing interest in creating an account.

Inpatient Enrollment by the Numbers

From the program start date of March 2015 to July 2017, the Library has coordinated a total of 2904 volunteer hours and approached patients 6638 times. Of these encounters, 70.9% resulted in a patient decline to receive a welcome email, 24.7% resulted in a welcome email being sent, and 4.5% resulted in a portal account being created for the patient while the volunteer was present. The reasons for decline, as noted by the volunteers were lack of computer ability (20.3%), inability to speak English (21.2%), limited computer or Internet access (17.3%), or other (28.4%). The other category reflected mostly a generalized lack of interest.

OUTPATIENT ENGAGEMENT

The Library also worked with an interdisciplinary group to implement the portal across the Network's outpatient clinics. These efforts were focused primarily on 13 primary care clinics in the Network. Given the diverse and geographically distributed nature of each of the primary and specialty care clinics, the Library's main role in patient enrollment was as a support to the clinics, as each sought to offer access to the greatest number of patients. In the initial phase, the Library attended regular Network-wide meetings to conduct train-the-trainer sessions on how to enroll patients. Through this role, the Library identified successful workflows developed at individual clinics and shared them across the Network. For example, several clinics implemented a workflow in which all front desk staff were instructed to assess patient interest in patient portal registration during the patient check-in process. Interested patients were sent a welcome email, and noninterested patients were marked as a decline (an important metric for meeting Meaningful Use requirements). Although this approach was more comprehensive and potentially avoided some disparities in portal access, it was not feasible at some sites because of high patient volume and relatively low staffing levels. Additionally, individualized support for patients with setting up an email account and creating their patient portal login was not possible in the clinic setting as a result of staffing constraints.

Staff Training

Following site visits and trainings at Network-wide meetings and several visits to individual clinics, the Library hosted three train-the-trainer sessions for "Patient Portal Clinic Champions" covering (1) the provisioning process (2) patient interaction scripts, (3) patient educational materials, and (4) strategies for implementation in the clinic setting. These "Clinic Champions" were then responsible for incorporating the training in their respective clinics for local enhancement and management.

The Library then followed up with site visits to clinics requesting further information and on-site trainings for their entire staff. These visits also provided the clinics with an opportunity to report success and challenges and for the Library to better respond to the diverse needs of the patients and clinics in the Network as a whole.

Portal Enrollment Competition

To further incentivize clinic adoption and patient enrollment, the Library worked alongside the Patient Engagement Workgroup to coordinate a clinic competition, in which 13 primary care clinics' enrollment numbers (patient enrollment/total number of eligible patient visits and improvement over time) were tracked monthly by hospital administration and distributed to the clinics via a shared dashboard. At the request of the clinics, the Workgroup partnered with a graphic designer to create updated and translated portal promotion materials, including trifolds and pamphlets for outpatient settings. Three prizes of pizza parties for clinic staff were funded by central Network administration—for best overall, most improved by percent, and most improved in comparison with baseline.

The clinics with the lowest enrollment metrics at the competition start had the highest rates of improvement, suggesting the competition model may be most helpful for starting new or less-developed patient portal enrollment programs. Overall, on the outpatient side, from go live in December 2014 to the end of August 2017, a total of 22,365 patients were sent a welcome email, and 8775 logged in.

RESEARCH MODELS

The Library worked across disciplines to research and develop more effective ways to engage underserved patients with patient portal systems. The library director served as co-principal investigator on a grant, "Overcoming Health Disparities by Engaging Patients with the Personal Health Record" funded by the National Library of Medicine through a G08 Grant to Information Resource Grant to Reduce Health Disparities (NIH Grant_1G08LM012166). The grant had three specific aims: (1) develop an evidence-based patient portal curriculum co-designed by patients (2) conduct a formal evaluation of this curriculum, and (3) test the curriculum template's scalability and sustainability across other sites.

The Need for Patient Portal Curriculum for the Underserved

This project draws from previous research by the Patient Engagement Workgroup, suggesting a need for patient portal curriculum for low-health literacy patients. In a series of in-depth interviews, the Workgroup found patients access the Internet at home and in libraries for a wide range of tasks, and they have a high level of interest in using patient portal systems to access their health information online. Yet in subsequent "think aloud" interviews, in which participants were asked to express their thoughts as they navigated the patient portal interface, it was found many patients had difficulty using the patient portal, including using a secure password, and navigating the portal's user interface. This suggested a need for trainings to address these barriers and other challenges patients may encounter.[27]

Advisory Groups

The Research Team consisting of the library director, faculty research partner, and research analyst established two advisory groups, which met separately over a 2-year period, to help conceptualize and iterate the patient portal curriculum and research approach. The first was a patient advisory group made up of patients and caregivers from the health-care system, and the second was an interdisciplinary project advisory group comprising librarians, clinicians, health informatics leadership, literacy researchers, and nonprofit employees focused on technology literacy.

Video-Based Curriculum

With the advisory boards' input, the Research Team developed a video-based curriculum consisting of 11 short videos, each 2–3 min in length. Nine of the video modules focused on showing patients how to complete specific tasks in the portal interface. These tasks included signing up, signing in, how to retrieve a forgotten password or username, navigating the homepage, viewing the visit summary, viewing the personal health record summary, viewing laboratory results, and looking up information in the online library. Two video modules focused more broadly on communicating the benefits of using the portal. In the first, a patient shares her personal story about how she uses the portal to manage her health. In the second, a physician provider communicates the importance of a portal website to improve care and communication.

Testing the Curriculum

Following the creation of the videos, the Research Team recruited 93 patients from two primary care clinics to participate in the grant study. Participants had to be English speaking, have a chronic health condition, a recent clinic visit, previous email use, and no extensive prior portal use. Participants were randomized into one of two arms, the first received an in-person tutorial with a trained research assistant and the second received a link to watch the videos without a trainer present. Using back end portal usage data provided by Hospital administration, the Research Team then measured portal enrollment and logins following the training with the two groups. The Research Team also measured perceptions of (1) portal importance and usefulness, (2) experience with chronic illness health care and self-management, and (3) ratings of digital and health literacy via baseline surveys and follow-up surveys 3–6 months posttraining.

Overall, among the 93 participants, 18 participants (20.5%) logged in to the portal during the follow-up period, and 17 (19.5%) initiated sign-up in their clinic. Proportions of sign-up and login did not differ by the in-person versus take-home training assignments. These rates of portal use of approximately 20% in each arm were substantially higher than the average portal use in the clinics during the same timeframe, with about 9% of primary care patients in these clinics logging on overall. This suggests training can increase portal engagement compared with usual care, but was not sufficient in getting a majority of underserved patients to use the website.

The complete results of this research will be published in forthcoming manuscripts and poster presentations. In the next phase, the Research Team will explore scalability and sustainability of patient portal curriculum across other sites.

BENEFITS OF COLLABORATION

Benefits of Collaboration from the Library's Perspective

The patient portal project aligns with the Library's mission to connect patients and providers with high-quality information and allows for a scale and impact not possible through in-person interactions within the Library or at outreach events. With the portal project, the Library also gained project-driven access to a broad cross-section of the organization, a more nuanced understanding of the organization's structure, and greater visibility with administrators and other groups in the Hospital and Network.

The portal project also focuses the Library's research and grant-related activities. The Library was able to identify gaps in the literature and propose new research and grant-funded activities—specifically to create patient portal curriculums for the underserved. The grant application process and subsequent funding, in turn, catalyzed further collaborations with outside groups, such as the public library and community technology laboratories.

The library director also integrated the portal project into his own professional development and learning opportunities, including the UCSF Masters of Science in Healthcare Administration and Interprofessional Leadership and the National Library of Medicine/Association of Academic Health Sciences Libraries Leadership Fellowship Program[28]—both offered opportunities to refine patient portal project and research deliverables.

Benefits of Collaboration from the Health-Care System Perspective

For health-care systems serving disadvantaged populations, partnerships with health sciences libraries and librarians are a welcome collaboration, as health-care systems are always searching for new strategies to educate and empower patients to be engaged in their health. Health sciences librarians, given their significant expertise in patient education and communication, are uniquely positioned to lead a health technology and engagement intervention such as a patient portal. Librarians embedded within health-care systems serving safety-net populations understand the complex barriers patients face and are poised to address them directly through multifaceted approaches. Health sciences librarians not only have experience working with individual patients but also have experience in developing educational programs for underserved populations, generally including technical skills such as Internet and computer literacy. Librarians are program managers and have experience in business administration. Lastly, librarians have partnerships with other community organizations, and thus can extend the reach of patient engagement in health care more broadly. The collaboration between clinical champions and the Library has been highly successful for the development, implementation, promotion, and maintenance of the patient portal.

Benefits of Collaboration from the Researcher's Perspective

Partnering with Library staff and other community-based organizations can greatly expand the audience for disseminating key research findings. This includes increased opportunity for interaction with community groups and citizens directly, as well as providing new avenues for raising attention about projects with local policy makers or other key stakeholders. Furthermore, there are unique strengths of library leadership and staff that can enhance the impact of health-focused intervention, especially in terms of deep expertise in adult educational approaches complementary to the content knowledge among researchers. Finally, this type of partnership allows health researchers to expand their funding sources to include agencies interested in social programs to benefit communities, such as the Institute for Museum and Library Studies, rather than health-specific institutes alone, such as the National Institutes of Health.

Benefits of Collaboration from the Patients' Perspective

Patients, anonymously interviewed via research focus groups and trainings, also expressed their appreciation for the patient portal project. For example, this patient highlighted how a patient portal puts the patient at the center of the health-care process: "It's just the right thing to do. It's a discovery for medicine, I think, for helping the patients. I think that you get closer to us this way. Closer between doctors and patients. It brings patients right front and center."—Anonymous quote.

Caregivers described how the patient portal made their jobs more manageable:

> *[As a caregiver], I am constantly saving everything in sight. He is on so many different medications. Finding-wise, it can get out of control. The amount, the volume is so much…. If it is on the website, I can recycle everything the pharmacist and doctor gives.—Anonymous quote.*

Patients also described how a patient portal helped them improve their interactions with their providers, by helping them prepare before their visits, and learning more about their conditions after visits are finished. "[If] I had a consultation with my pharmacist and they're telling me of the side effects to watch out with some medications I'm taking [and] I have one of those side effects, I might discuss it with a doctor on email. That would be really helpful."—Anonymous quote. A patient also said,

> *The doctor tells me a lot, but a lot of it I don't understand and I think I could read more about it because they're always in a rush at the hospital with so many people waiting in the clinic. The computer can give me more information than the doctor can give me during the 15 minutes that they see me.—Anonymous quote.*

While some patients thought the portal's user interface was "clean and user-friendly,"—Anonymous quote, another patient expressed "it was kind of tough (to use) but I had never used it before so that's why it was tough. If I get used to doing it, it won't be so tough."—Anonymous quote. This points to the potential role for librarians to provide more training and education reflecting patients' perspectives and learning needs.

NEXT STEPS

There are many opportunities to build on this patient portal project to develop programs and services to engage patients with their health information through technology. The Library's space, which is near the Hospital and its on-site community clinics, has allowed it to serve as a hub for volunteers, team members, researchers, and patients to collaborate on patient portal projects and education. The Library can now build on its patient portal experience to form collaborations and offer in-person patient education for a broader range of patient facing platforms, technologies, and interventions.

CONCLUSION AND LESSONS LEARNED

Health Sciences librarians have a compelling mission to empower patrons to make evidence-based decisions. By engaging patients with their health information and health-care decisions, patient portals offer a powerful platform to put this mission into action at a scale not possible through in-person interactions. In conclusion, here is a list of the Patient Engagement Workgroup's lessons learned, for librarians looking to increase collaboration, as well as the impact of their resources and services.

1. Understand your vision and mission are distinct from your programs, resources, and activities. Look to see if your vision and mission would be more effectively advanced through new initiatives and partnerships, particularly at a system-wide level.
2. Align your projects around your institution's emerging or redefined program areas. Particularly, in lesser-resourced settings, institutions often rely on departments and staff to volunteer to initiate and give structure to new program areas.
3. Pursue your own grant funding. Funding opportunities are a powerful catalyst for assembling interdisciplinary teams to come together and form new ideas. The person who identifies the funding opportunity, proposes the initial concept, and assembles the key team members is often the de facto principal investigator, or co-principal investigator for the grant.
4. Build genuine relationships with your collaborators. People from diverse disciplines and department areas often share the same underlying objectives. Successful collaboration toward these objectives can span multiple projects and program areas, both large and small.

REFERENCES

1. Institute of Medicine. *America's Health Care Safety Net: Intact but Endangered.* Washington, DC: The National Academies Press; 2000. https://doi.org/10.17.
2. *What Is a Patient Portal?* Office of the National Coordinator for Health Information Technology; November 2015. Available from: https://www.healthit.gov/providers-professionals/faqs/what-patient-portal.

3. Ronda MC, Dijkhorst-Oei LT, Rutten GE. Patients' experiences with and attitudes towards a diabetes patient web portal. *PLoS One*. 2015;10(6):e0129403. Epub 2015/06/19 10.1371/journal.pone.0129403. PubMed PMID: 26086272; PubMed Central PMCID: PMC4472519.
4. Irizarry T, DeVito Dabbs A, Curran CR. Patient portals and patient engagement: a state of the science review. *J Med Internet Res*. 2015;17(6):e148. Epub 2015/06/25 10.2196/jmir.4255. PubMed PMID: 26104044; PubMed Central PMCID: PMC4526960.
5. Groen WG, Kuijpers W, Oldenburg HS, Wouters MW, Aaronson NK, van Harten WH. Empowerment of cancer survivors through information technology: an integrative review. *J Med Internet Res*. 2015;17(11):e270. Epub 2015/11/29 10.2196/jmir.4818. PubMed PMID: 26614438; PubMed Central PMCID: PMC4704924.
6. Bruno MA, Petscavage-Thomas JM, Mohr MJ, Bell SK, Brown SD. The "open letter": Radiologists' reports in the era of patient web portals. *J Am Coll Radiol*. 2014;11(9):863–867. Epub 2014/05/20 10.1016/j.jacr.2014.03.014. PubMed PMID: 24836272.
7. Kruse CS, Bolton K, Freriks G. The effect of patient portals on quality outcomes and its implications to meaningful use: a systematic review. *J Med Internet Res*. 2015;17(2):e44. Epub 2015/02/12 10.2196/jmir.3171. PubMed PMID: 25669240; PubMed Central PMCID: PMC4342639.
8. Patel V, Barker W, Siminerio E. *Office of the National Coordinator Data Brief: Individuals' Access and Use of Their Online Medical Record Nationwide*. Office of the National Coordinator; September 2014. Available from: https://www.healthit.gov/sites/default/files/consumeraccessdatabrief_9_10_14.pdf.
9. Tenforde M, Nowacki A, Jain A, Hickner J. The association between personal health record use and diabetes quality measures. *J Gen Intern Med*. 2012;27(4):420–424. Epub 2011/10/19 10.1007/s11606-011-1889-0. PubMed PMID: 22005937; PubMed Central PMCID: PMC3304034.
10. Ralston JD, Carrell D, Reid R, Anderson M, Moran M, Hereford J. Patient web services integrated with a shared medical record: patient use and satisfaction. *J Am Med Inform Assoc*. 2007;14(6):798–806. Epub 2007/08/23 10.1197/jamia.M2302. PubMed PMID: 17712090; PubMed Central PMCID: PMC2213480.
11. Sarkar U, Lyles CR, Parker MM, et al. Use of the refill function through an online patient portal is associated with improved adherence to statins in an integrated health system. *Med Care*. 2014;52(3):194–201. Epub 2014/01/01 10.1097/MLR.0000000000000069. PubMed PMID: 24374412; PubMed Central PMCID: PMC4005993.
12. Goldzweig CL, Orshansky G, Paige NM, et al. Electronic patient portals: evidence on health outcomes, satisfaction, efficiency, and attitudes: a systematic review. *Ann Intern Med*. 2013;159(10):677–687. Epub 2013/11/20 10.7326/0003-4819-159-10-201311190-00006. PubMed PMID: 24247673.
13. Blumenthal D. Launching HITECH. *N Engl J Med*. 2010;362(5):382–385. Epub 2010/01/01 10.1056/NEJMp0912825. PubMed PMID: 20042745.
14. Sullivan T. *Meaningful Use Incentives Step toward $25 Billion*. HealthcareITNews; July 10, 2014. Available from: http://www.healthcareitnews.com/news/meaningful-use-incentives-step-toward-25-billion.
15. Blumenthal D, Tavenner M. The "meaningful use" regulation for electronic health records. *N Engl J Med*. 2010;363(6):501–504. Epub 2010/07/22 10.1056/NEJMp1006114. PubMed PMID: 20647183.
16. Perc M. The Matthew Effect in empirical data. *J R Soc Interface*. 2014;11(98):20140378. Epub 2014/07/06 10.1098/rsif.2014.0378. PubMed PMID: 24990288; PubMed Central PMCID: PMCPMC4233686.

17. Sarkar U, Karter AJ, Liu JY, et al. The literacy divide: health literacy and the use of an internet-based patient portal in an integrated health system-results from the diabetes study of northern California (DISTANCE). *J Health Commun.* 2010;15(Suppl 2):183–196. Epub 2010/09/29 10.1080/10810730.2010.499988. PubMed PMID: 20845203; PubMed Central PMCID: PMC3014858.
18. Sarkar U, Karter AJ, Liu JY, et al. Social disparities in internet patient portal use in diabetes: evidence that the digital divide extends beyond access. *J Am Med Inform Assoc.* 2011;18(3):318–321. Epub 2011/01/26 10.1136/jamia.2010.006015. PubMed PMID: 21262921; PubMed Central PMCID: PMC3078675.
19. Goel MS, Brown TL, Williams A, Hasnain-Wynia R, Thompson JA, Baker DW. Disparities in enrollment and use of an electronic patient portal. *J Gen Intern Med.* 2011;26(10):1112–1116. Epub 2011/05/04 10.1007/s11606-011-1728-3. PubMed PMID: 21538166; PubMed Central PMCID: PMC3181306.
20. Smith SG, O'Conor R, Aitken W, Curtis LM, Wolf MS, Goel MS. Disparities in registration and use of an online patient portal among older adults: findings from the LitCog cohort. *J Am Med Inform Assoc.* 2015;22(4):888–895. Epub 2015/04/29 10. 1093/jamia/ocv025. PubMed PMID: 25914099; PubMed Central PMCID: PMC4810779.
21. Wallace LS, Angier H, Huguet N, et al. Patterns of electronic portal use among vulnerable patients in a nationwide practice-based research network: from the OCHIN Practice-Based Research Network (PBRN). *J Am Board Fam Med.* 2016;29(5):592–603. Epub 2016/09/11 10.3122/jabfm.2016.05.160046. PubMed PMID: 27613792; PubMed Central PMCID: PMC5341130.
22. Lyles CR, Harris LT, Jordan L, et al. Patient race/ethnicity and shared medical record use among diabetes patients. *Med Care.* 2012;50(5):434–440. Epub 2012/02/23 10. 1097/MLR.0b013e318249d81b. PubMed PMID: 22354209.
23. Brach C, Keller D, Hernandez LM, et al. *Ten Attributes of Health Literate Health Care Organizations.* Washington, DC: Institute of Medicine; 2012. Available from: https://nam.edu/wp-content/uploads/2015/06/BPH_Ten_HLit_Attributes.pdf.
24. *About Community Technology Network.* Community Technology Network; 2017. Available from: https://www.communitytechnetwork.org/about/.
25. *Project Read.* San Francisco Public Library; 2017. Available from: https://sfpl.org/?pg=2000886801.
26. *Plan-Do-Study-Act (PDSA) Worksheet.* Cambridge, MA: Institute for Healthcare Improvement; 2014. Available from: http://www.ihi.org/resources/Pages/Tools/PlanDoStudyActWorksheet.aspx.
27. Tieu L, Schillinger D, Sarkar U, et al. Online patient websites for electronic health record access among vulnerable populations: portals to nowhere? *J Am Med Inform Assoc.* 2017;24(e1):e47–e54. Epub 2016/07/13 10.1093/jamia/ocw098. PubMed PMID: 27402138.
28. *NLM/AAHSL Leadership Fellows Program.* Seattle: Association of Academic Health Sciences Libraries; 2017. Available from: https://www.aahsl.org/leadershipfellows.

CHAPTER 4

Finding the Way Without a Road MAP: Cultivating a UK-Wide Community of Practice

Tracey Pratchett[1], Victoria Treadway[2]
[1]Knowledge and Library Services Manager, Lancashire Teaching Hospitals NHS Foundation Trust, Preston, United Kingdom; [2]Library and Knowledge Service Lead, Wirral University Teaching Hospital NHS Foundation Trust, Wirral, United Kingdom

INTRODUCTION

This chapter shares the experience of establishing and participating in a Community of Practice (CoP) among library professionals, the output of which is the Making Alignment a Priority (MAP) Toolkit.[1] The toolkit provides a bank of resources enabling libraries in the National Health Service (NHS) in England to demonstrate value and impact. This chapter discusses the evolution of the CoP in response to the challenges facing the NHS in England. Library professionals engaged in the MAP CoP share learning with each other, while making this learning available to the wider health sciences library community via the MAP Toolkit available online via a Wordpress blog. The effect of this collective learning and the MAP Toolkit on those immersed in the CoP and the wider health sciences library profession is explored. Applications of theoretical principles from the literature relating to CoP are considered. Recommendations for other library professionals interested in adopting a similar approach conclude the chapter.

BACKGROUND TO THE NHS

Since its inception in 2008, the MAP CoP has operated against an ever-changing political backdrop. Its members work in libraries based in different organizations in the NHS in England. The NHS is publicly funded and provides health services free at the point of need for the population in England. NHS libraries are funded by organizations to provide services to clinical and management teams and students on placement and are therefore influenced by changes in government policy. Library professionals need to

Strategic Collaborations in Health Sciences Libraries
ISBN 978-0-08-102258-0
https://doi.org/10.1016/B978-0-08-102258-0.00004-5
Copyright © 2019 Jean P. Shipman and M.J. Tooey. Published by Elsevier Limited. All rights reserved.

remain abreast of emerging political drivers, both in a national and local context. This can sometimes prove challenging for librarians as a result of information overload, lack of time, and difficulty in translating high-level policy documents into meaningful language for the library sector.

Since 2008 there have been many changes to the NHS landscape, perhaps most notably, the 2012 Health & Social Care Act [2] which saw the complete reorganization of health-care services across England. More recently, efforts have been made to explore ways in which the NHS can collaborate more effectively across organizational boundaries through the creation of Sustainability and Transformation Partnerships.[3] The result of this is increased partnership among NHS trusts and NHS foundation trusts, the organizations responsible for the delivery of health care in England. In some cases entire organizations have merged. For example, the creation of Manchester University NHS Foundation Trust brought Central Manchester NHS Foundation Trust and University Hospitals of South Manchester together into one organization. These changes have made a significant impact on libraries operating in the NHS resulting in not only the user base being completely altered but also creating changes in the strategic priorities of the organization.

LIBRARIES IN THE NHS

Libraries in the NHS support health-care professionals' educational requirements and provide evidence to underpin service delivery. Organizational mergers have resulted in a reduction in the number of NHS libraries across England. In 2014, there were 215 libraries offering services to the NHS in England.[4] This number has been reduced by 5% at the time of writing, and this downward trend may continue. Libraries have different strategic objectives dependent on the population served. For example, libraries within an acute hospital have different priorities and deliver different services from those serving a mental health service or public health team.

There are several reasons why it is necessary for libraries in NHS England to demonstrate their contribution to their host organization. Library funding in NHS England is complex, dependent on host organizations, creating staffing and service delivery inconsistencies across the country. For organizations, mainly hospitals, receiving funding from Health Education England (HEE) to provide training placements for students, there is a contractual requirement outlined in the Learning Development Agreement to provide a Library Service.[5] However, not all health libraries are based in training organizations and for these there is no legal requirement to provide services; therefore, the survival of these libraries is dependent on the ability to demonstrate value and impact.

Justifying investment in NHS libraries is a driving force behind the need to demonstrate value. NHS organizations have been challenged to make efficiency savings and deliver effective services while working more collaboratively with other health-care providers.[3] Within this context of restructuring and cost improvement, there is an increasing need for libraries to demonstrate the impact they make upon strategic objectives to ensure their survival.

ORIGINS OF THE MAP COP

The challenge to demonstrate value and impact was the key driver for librarians in NHS England to come together as the MAP CoP in 2008, with the aim to equip themselves with the tools to meet this challenge. At that time, the concept that NHS libraries should need to demonstrate their alignment with NHS priorities was a novel one, and there were few resources available to support librarians in doing this.

The MAP CoP originated in North West England, when eight librarians came together inspired by a London-based collaboration: the LondonLinks Alignment Project.[6] Two of the founding MAP members attended a showcase event where different types of health libraries in London presented case studies demonstrating the unique impact of services in the context of two political drivers: the Darzi Quality Review[7] and the Hill Review.[8]

Lord Darzi's report, published in 2008, signaled a shift for the NHS from performance and targets to a focus on quality. The report defined quality in relation to patient experience, patient safety, and patient care. Peter Hill's review, also published in 2008, outlined the "centrality of library services" in the delivery of excellent health care. The review outlined four central purposes for libraries—supporting clinical decision-making, commissioning (planning, agreeing, and monitoring health services),[9] research, and lifelong learning in the NHS. The LondonLinks librarians aligned their case studies to these drivers, powerfully demonstrating how Hill's recommendations were met, while making a direct impact on the one thing that mattered most to leaders in their organizations: the quality of patient care.

The MAP CoP came together to discuss how a similarly powerful collection of case studies might be created for the North West of England. Following a series of in-depth discussions it became clear that NHS organizations (and therefore NHS libraries) were being influenced by various different national priorities, or "drivers" in addition to those identified by the LondonLinks Project. The idea that there are numerous local and national priorities simultaneously influencing NHS organizations became a key focus for the MAP CoP. To demonstrate impact effectively, it was vital that library professionals have a clear understanding of the priorities that were driving NHS organizations and their implications for library services.

The MAP CoP met many times to shape its aim, which was twofold: to help NHS librarians to understand local, regional, and national NHS priorities and to enable them to showcase examples of library impact aligned with these priorities. The CoP decided to create an online toolkit (MAP Toolkit) to host the resources it intended to produce: summaries of significant NHS policies and case studies of instances where NHS libraries had aligned their services successfully with NHS priorities.

Since 2008 the requirement to demonstrate impact has been addressed by the national program for NHS libraries in England: the Knowledge for Healthcare Development Framework.[4] One of the work streams included created a Value and Impact toolkit and repository of impact case studies. To complement this coordinated approach, a campaign was launched in 2017 by the Chartered Institute of Library and Information Professionals (CILIP) and HEE.[10] The campaign, A Million Decisions, presented a vision of a truly evidence-based health service. Through this campaign, stories about the contribution libraries make to NHS organizations were shared in the mainstream media. In its 2017 policy, HEE outlined its vision to provide "free at the point of need" libraries for the health-care workforce, asserting a role for library professionals in mobilizing organizational knowledge and promoting the delivery of a national, coherent library service for the NHS.[11] The MAP CoP had emerged in 2008 as a librarian response to a local need to demonstrate impact and alignment with NHS objectives; it has since evolved to work alongside national programs with the same aim emerging later.

THE EVOLUTION OF THE MAP COP

Communities of practice often evolve spontaneously around groups of people with similar interests, concerns, or passions.[12] In the case of the MAP CoP, the original members came together with a shared vision: a showcase of impactful stories about libraries aligned to the priorities, or drivers, of their organizations. The original CoP included eight library professionals, each based in a different health-care organization. The original MAP CoP was united in its passion and vision, which evolved over time, adapting to changing health-care priorities.

The current MAP CoP has evolved significantly from its early incarnation; it now includes 10 members from across England and is seeking additional members from across the United Kingdom. Membership has broadened to include library professionals from outside the NHS, with a library professional from the public library sector joining the membership. The CoP developed organically. New members are recruited at events and via a number of email distribution lists. The CoP membership has changed as people join and leave, introducing different perspectives and skills. Although there are no formal roles, unofficial roles have emerged according to individual skills and preferences. The original members act as the CoP leads. Membership includes a technical lead who troubleshoots problems with Wordpress, and a public relations lead who is responsible for writing short promotional pieces for email discussion lists, and newsletters for the wider health library communities, such as the *Health Libraries Group Newsletter*.[13] Despite membership changes, the aim of the MAP CoP remains constant: supporting library professionals in demonstrating the impact of their services. Consistency in leadership has undoubtedly enabled the CoP to sustain its original vision while exploiting the new ideas, skills, and experiences of newer community members.

Integral to any CoP is learning. Learning occurs when members share their experiences, discuss problems, and use expertise to learn from one another. The MAP CoP is no different; members meet regularly to reflect on experiences, share progress, and agree on future directions. Library professionals from the wider health sciences library community interact with the CoP by suggesting new drivers and contributing completed project plans and case studies which are then made available online via the MAP Toolkit. In this way, the MAP CoP captures the knowledge of its members and the wider health sciences library community, repackaging it for the benefit of a wider library audience.

The MAP CoP is not driven by an external organizational or policy agenda, but is influenced by the interests and desires of the CoP members. The MAP CoP supports its members, and while members have informal roles according to specializations or areas of interest, there is no defined hierarchy. The authors of this chapter are the original members, originators and "thought leaders" who help to maintain focus, develop a shared direction, and sustain momentum.[12]

The MAP CoP communicates with the wider health sciences library community using existing library networks and communication channels, including social media, email discussion lists, conferences, and meetings. The MAP CoP meets virtually every 1–2 months using teleconferencing facilities. Regular face-to-face interaction is not possible with members dispersed across England. However, the CoP members meet annually, usually in Stafford, which is central to all members. The meeting agenda is developed collectively and the informal annual meeting allows a more in-depth exploration of key issues. An action plan is developed for the coming year. This face-to-face meeting is beneficial for old and new members of the CoP providing an opportunity to nurture working relationships, enabling deeper learning, and providing a forum to agree on future directions. The opportunity to meet face-to-face allows members to develop trusting relationships, which are difficult to maintain when all interactions operate virtually.[14]

THE MAP TOOLKIT

The aim of the MAP Toolkit is to host resources online to enable library professionals to successfully demonstrate alignment with NHS priorities. The MAP Toolkit is the main output from the MAP CoP. It is an online platform hosted on the free version of Wordpress.[1] The platform has had a number of incarnations, initially being hosted on a closed PBWorks wiki, and only made available to library professionals based in the North West upon request.

Although this model enabled the community to monitor membership and usage, it also presented a barrier to new users and inhibited engagement within the wider health sciences library community. Content was transferred to a Wordpress blog in 2013, providing flexibility for the central MAP Toolkit Team, and improving accessibility as it does not require a login. The MAP Toolkit on Wordpress is open access. Users are alerted when new content is added and it has an average of 568 views per month. There are still some perceived disadvantages to using Wordpress, which will be discussed in more detail later in this chapter.

One of the challenges faced by the CoP is that membership is voluntary with no funding to support its work. The development of the toolkit was initially supported by individual organizations with some funding from the Library and Information Health Network Northwest[15]; however, there has never been a central funding source. The CoP is reliant on freely available software to develop the toolkit and host online content.

The toolkit contains a range of tools and templates available for any library professional to use when planning their services in a way that demonstrates impact on NHS priorities. This includes:

- Driver summaries: easy to read, digestible summaries of key health and social care policies, reports and publications, translated for a library audience.
- Evidence summaries and hot topics: Summaries of subjects that are current or topical in the NHS that can be disseminated to health-care professionals via library services.
- Ideas Capture template: an informal project planning tool for library professionals to capture thoughts and ideas at the outset of project development.
- MAP Stories template: a case study template for library professionals to write up and share impactful stories illustrating how library services have contributed to NHS priorities.
- Examples of library service documentation including annual reports, library strategies and completed MAP Stories, to share good practice and inspire other library professionals.
- Blog posts written by members of the CoP reflecting on ideas and experiences relating to impact.

The toolkit is updated and developed by all members of the CoP, with contributions from the wider health sciences library community on an ad hoc basis. The CoP encourages contributions from other library professionals particularly when additional expertise is required. For example, library professionals from mental health and public health organizations have written driver summaries relevant to their area of expertise for addition to the toolkit.

A primary element of the toolkit is the collection of driver summaries. A driver may be a newly published report, piece of legislation, a national policy, or project which is of significance to the NHS. All members of the MAP CoP scan for potential new drivers via mailing lists, social media, meetings, and informal networks. Drivers are summarized by CoP members in a digestible format enabling the reader to quickly understand the key points. The summary examines the implications of the driver for NHS library services and suggests how libraries might support their home organizations in working toward this driver. Librarians who follow the MAP Toolkit via the blog or Twitter are notified when a new driver summary has been published. In this way the MAP Toolkit acts as an alerting service for library professionals.

One specific example illustrates the process of summarizing drivers' works in practice. In 2015 the UK Nursing and Midwifery Council (NMC) introduced mandatory revalidation for nurses in the NHS. The originating report was added to the drivers section of the toolkit.[16] The report asserted that nurses in the United Kingdom needed to ensure that they were producing reflective portfolios and undertaking relevant training. It was an opportunity for library services to support nurses with revalidation by providing information skills training and support with reflective writing. By aligning the delivery of library services with this mandatory requirement by the NMC, libraries were presented as responsive and vital services to their organization, while also speaking the same language as NHS leaders and decision-makers. The MAP Toolkit supported this endeavor by summarizing the lengthy document produced by the NMC for a library audience and suggesting ways that library services could support implementation of this new mandatory requirement.[17]

Driver summaries remain on the MAP Toolkit while they are still relevant providing a searchable archive as a reference tool for library professionals. The CoP reviews driver summaries annually to ensure the MAP Toolkit content remains current in the ever-changing NHS landscape. Outdated drivers are removed when no longer of relevance.[18] The archive is particularly helpful for library professionals who are writing library strategies, providing easy access to key drivers and summary of their relevance to library services.

Library professionals from the wider health sciences library community sometimes suggest potential new drivers to the MAP CoP. These are sent to the CoP to be shared via the online toolkit as a resource for the wider health sciences library community, thus reducing duplication and supporting a "do once and share" approach.

The MAP Toolkit includes a collection of downloadable templates to support library professionals in project planning and writing case studies in a way that aligns their work with NHS drivers. Each template is accompanied by guidance encouraging the writer to align their work with key priorities for the NHS. The aim is to provide tools that library professionals may use to plan their services with the wider NHS context in mind and to present their work as integral to the objectives and priorities driving their organization. MAP templates were renamed in 2016, harnessing more imaginative and informal language to encourage accessibility. The project plan template was renamed to "Ideas Capture" and the case study template was renamed "MAP Stories." These changes were made following feedback from new members of the CoP.

The CoP encourages library professionals who have used the templates to share their completed documents on the toolkit, enabling the sharing of good practice with other NHS libraries. The toolkit also includes examples of library strategies and annual reports produced and shared by library professionals from the wider health sciences library community. This section of the toolkit is popular and is used by library professionals looking for inspiration when creating their own reports and strategies.

The MAP CoP has collaborated with other programs pursuing the shared aim of demonstrating the impact of NHS libraries. In 2014, a small number of "knowledge management stories," sourced by a colleague from an NHS library, were added to the toolkit. The stories describe instances where Library and Knowledge Services (LKS) staff built networks within their organizations and made connections between people and the knowledge they needed. In 2016 these stories were combined with other knowledge management stories captured from the wider health sciences library community as part of the Knowledge for Healthcare program and transferred to a new platform, the Knowledge for Healthcare blog.[19] In this way, duplication was avoided by ensuring that all knowledge management case studies were stored in a central location.

Recent developments in NHS library services have prompted the MAP CoP to ensure that its content remains relevant to the needs of library professionals. The fast-paced nature of health and social care in NHS England means that library services are increasingly being called upon to support NHS leaders in understanding national policy changes. The CoP has responded to this call by creating and publishing evidence summaries of current NHS "hot topics," which are emerging new priority areas for NHS managers. For example, a "hot topic" summary describing Accountable Care Organizations has been added to the toolkit, explaining how they are influencing the direction of health-care delivery in NHS England.[20] This content positions the MAP Toolkit as a responsive, alerting resource for library professionals.

The MAP Toolkit content requires regular promotion so that new content can reach the hundreds of busy library professionals working across the United Kingdom. New content is promoted using an MAP Twitter account (@map_community) and quarterly bulletins are disseminated via email discussion lists and newsletters to reach the wider health sciences library community. Members of the CoP speak at conferences and events and facilitate workshops around England to promote use of the toolkit. Continual promotion ensures that the MAP Toolkit remains visible to library professionals and helps in recruiting additional members.

WHY ARE COMMUNITIES OF PRACTICE IMPORTANT TO LIBRARIANS?

Communities of practice are valuable to librarians, contributing to the development of social capital, necessary for knowledge creation, sharing, and use.[14] Library professionals across all sectors find value in communities of practice as they provide opportunities for collaboration with other practitioners and stakeholders. Organizational communities of practice provide opportunities for library professionals to collaborate with nonlibrary teams within the organization. Collective expertise is brought together to solve problems or generate knowledge. For example, at Lancashire Teaching Hospitals, librarians are part of a Research Development Group including representatives from the organization's research team, statisticians, and members of the public. The function of this particular CoP is to share research expertise with individuals wishing to pursue a research idea or become research-active. The group also exists to progress a key aim of the organization: to develop the research capability of its staff and encourage research output.

Communities of practice sometimes also emerge within larger libraries. In the academic sector, community members often come together from different library teams.[14] These communities can exploit the expertise and enthusiasm existing within different teams by providing opportunities for people to work together on projects, such as developing a website or exploring emerging technologies. As most health libraries in England are small teams, usually with fewer than 10 staff, it is difficult for internal communities of practice to operate in this way.

Library professionals in NHS England have historically been part of networks and communities of practice according to region. Although this network structure was geographically practical, it didn't necessarily allow for effective sharing of expertise across England as a whole. In 2015, HEE, the organization responsible for leading workforce training and education in NHS England, launched a development framework for NHS libraries, titled Knowledge for Healthcare. Knowledge for Healthcare aims to take a strategic, national approach to delivering NHS library services. Knowledge for Healthcare work streams are undertaken by librarians across England who are coordinating national projects in several different areas. The result of this is the emergence of collaborative groups of like-minded library professionals, driven by their own areas of interest and expertise rather than geographic proximity. Over 60 projects are currently being advanced by communities of library professionals working across organizational boundaries. These communities of practice bring together individuals with shared interests and expertise to deliver resources and support for librarians across the whole country. Knowledge for Healthcare work streams cover the following areas:

- Value and Impact
- Patient and Public Health Information
- Knowledge Management
- Talent Management
- Developing the Library Workforce
- Service Transformation[21]

This national approach taken by the Knowledge for Healthcare Development Framework ensures that expertise is harnessed from knowledgeable library professionals across NHS England to progress and improve service delivery for the entire sector. Similarly, the MAP CoP brings together like-minded librarians for the benefit of the wider profession. So not only do library communities of practice enable librarians to broaden their individual knowledge base and improve the delivery of their local library services, they also enable advancement of the profession as a whole.

Communities of practice allow the expertise, ideas, and experiences of like-minded individuals to be harnessed and shared. Even volunteer communities of practice enhance motivation and capture the enthusiasm of the individuals involved. The MAP CoP brings people together from different organizations, presenting a rich-learning experience for participants to develop skills outside of their daily environment. Communities of practice delivering the Knowledge for Healthcare vision enable a number of projects to be pursued at low cost for the benefit of the entire health community.[21]

IMPACT OF BEING INVOLVED IN THE MAP COMMUNITY

Being a member of the MAP CoP enables librarians to broaden their own knowledge and skills, improve the services they deliver, and network with other library professionals working in other NHS organizations.

Members develop professional and technical skills by participating in the CoP; summarizing lengthy reports and adding them to the MAP Toolkit enables librarians to improve their summarizing and blogging skills. Members participate in a range of professional development activities: facilitating workshops, presenting at conferences, writing for publication, marketing, and promotion. Being part of a national CoP allows members to build their professional profile and reputation as leaders.

The CoP facilitates networking, connecting library professionals from different sectors and opposite ends of the country who would not have met otherwise. Although the main focus is on developing the toolkit, members also share ideas, reflections, and experiences that have enhanced their own service delivery. Often teleconference discussions digress and become a supportive forum for members to talk about professional issues.

Members have used resources on the MAP Toolkit to plan projects locally then share them with other library professionals by publishing them on the toolkit. In this way the CoP provides tools for members to improve their own library services while also acting as a mechanism for sharing good practice.

Members have developed their political and strategic awareness, helping them to understand the priorities influencing their own organizations. Members feel that this helps them to "speak the language" of senior leaders in their organizations, and this broadened understanding has helped members to write business cases, create and develop new services, and make connections within their organization.

IMPACT OF THE COMMUNITY ON THE WIDER LIBRARY COMMUNITY

The MAP Toolkit has been utilized by many others within the wider health sciences library sector to develop and enhance their own work. In 2011, Brettle et al. undertook a systematic review to consider the impact of clinical librarians on organizational objectives.[22] This review adapted MAP templates to evaluate services with regard to local, regional, and organizational policy drivers. A 2016 follow-up study to evaluate the impact of clinical librarians in the North West of England used the MAP Toolkit to identify policy drivers of relevance to clinical librarian services.[23]

Work streams progressing the Knowledge for Healthcare Development Framework have used the resources on the MAP Toolkit to underpin their work. One of the work streams, the Patient and Public Information Group, used MAP templates to produce its own summaries of NHS drivers, relating specifically to health consumer information.[24] Dan Livesy, LKS Manager at Greater Manchester Mental Health NHS Foundation Trust, stated that:

> *The MAP Toolkit templates and supporting information was invaluable for the Knowledge for Healthcare Patient and Public Information Group. The driver templates made it easy for us to summarize complex regulation and guidance. Our drivers are now available to support any NHS librarian who is thinking about impact or innovation, specifically around patient information.*

The MAP CoP has embraced the endeavors of the Knowledge for Healthcare work streams and embraced the opportunity for greater collaboration and learning. MAP has worked alongside one of these work streams, the Knowledge Management Group, producing a central repository of Knowledge Management Stories.[25] MAP CoP has shared resources and collaborated on workshops with another, the Value and Impact Group.[26] The Value and Impact work stream had significant crossover with the work of the CoP. Inspired by these similarities, the MAP CoP adapted the content of the toolkit to avoid unnecessary duplication focusing on sharing information about key policy drivers and hot topics rather than collecting case studies.

The MAP Toolkit has also been used by individual library professionals working across and beyond England. In 2017 there were 6505 hits on the website, originating from a range of countries including the United Kingdom, United States, Australia, and Ireland. In 2017, the toolkit was evaluated by distributing a survey via mailing lists to the wider health sciences library community to find how the toolkit was used, identifying areas for development. Of the 22 survey respondents from librarians working in health across the United Kingdom, 50% had used the toolkit up to five times in the past year. Discussion lists were the most effective mechanism for communicating updates from the MAP CoP and changes to the toolkit, highlighting the benefit of utilizing existing communication channels. When an update is issued, usage of the toolkit increases, statistics show a spike in activity occurring the week after the communication is issued, and an approximately 100% increase in hits is seen on the site when compared with the previous week.

Other library professionals have used the MAP Toolkit to develop business cases, produce case studies, and even reflect on their own professional development. Rebecca Roylance, information specialist at the University Hospital Aintree said:

> *We used the case study template to plan and monitor our current awareness service. It helped to consider all aspects before the project commenced, rather than just diving in and missing aspects. It helped to direct the project by considering why we were actually doing it, what objectives it aligned to. The reflection aspect of the template was really useful for determining the positive results of the project and what we could do differently next time.*

Recently, members of the MAP CoP have delivered workshops to library professionals allowing participants to explore the practical uses of the MAP templates, discuss barriers to collecting impact data, and to share ideas and innovations from their own library teams. Lis Edwards, Library Services Manager, The Robert Jones and Agnes Hunt Orthopaedic Hospital NHS Trust, commented:

> *Attending the MAP workshop helped me to identify how we can demonstrate how our service impacts on our organization.*
>
> *The case study template in particular gave me the structure to demonstrate how our event had delivered impact throughout the Trust.*

New members of the MAP CoP have also been recruited via these workshops, highlighting the need for the community to have a face-to-face presence with the wider health sciences library community and its online existence.

THE CHALLENGES

Since its inception in 2008, the MAP CoP has transformed from a local initiative to a national resource. It has survived membership changes, limited resources, and a turbulent political backdrop. However, there have been many challenges along the way.

Communication among the MAP CoP members, which consists of busy professionals contributing voluntarily, requires effort. After struggling to meet in person for many years because of time and travel constraints, virtual meetings are now hosted using webinar software allowing members to connect from the comfort of their workplace.

A consistent struggle has been to recruit and retain members to the MAP CoP. Involvement is an addition to day-to-day employment and the time commitment can be difficult for library professionals who are already busy and under pressure. The MAP CoP, therefore, has to be creative in the way it articulates the benefits of joining the community. It also means the community is composed of dedicated, motivated, and progressive library professionals who value being part of the venture.

The MAP CoP and toolkit have existed since 2008, and during this time, the emergence of the national vision for library services in NHS England, the Knowledge for Healthcare Development Framework, has overlapped with some of the MAP CoP work. Both initiatives share the desire to demonstrate the powerful impact of libraries within the wider NHS. Rather than working in isolation, the MAP community has worked alongside these other initiatives to avoid duplication of effort.

Lack of funding has been a constant challenge for the MAP CoP. The result of this is a reliance on freely available software such as Wordpress to host the MAP Toolkit. This means users are inundated with advertising. Wordpress is also inaccessible to some NHS libraries as a result of firewall restrictions operating in their organizations. If funding were available, a more robust website could be developed, accessible to all and with a more professional image.

Feedback from a 2017 survey of users of the MAP Toolkit suggested that the function of the MAP Toolkit in identifying new NHS priorities and policy changes is increasingly popular. The wider health sciences library community is thirsty for new content, wanting new drivers and national policy to be added to the toolkit as quickly as possible. If additional volunteers were recruited to the MAP CoP, new driver summaries could be published to the MAP Toolkit more quickly as the workload would be shared among a larger number of people.

CONCLUSIONS

The MAP CoP exists as a valuable forum for members to share experiences, ideas, and learning across organizational boundaries. It supports library professionals in the development of services and professional skills, while enabling them to demonstrate alignment with the strategic priorities of their home organizations. The MAP CoP has overcome various challenges of membership, resources, and politics, driven by the focus and motivation of its members.

For those wanting to adopt a similar approach, the experiences of the MAP CoP demonstrate the following as critical success factors in developing a CoP:

- A shared vision and ethos driven by a core membership.
- Resilience and flexibility during times of change.

- Creation and nurturing of an open and enjoyable forum appealing to potential members.
- Embracing of similar projects as an opportunity to widen collaboration.
- Use of existing networks and communication channels to encourage participation.

The learning supported by participation in the MAP CoP is invaluable, as are the development of professional skills. In a sector where learning "on the job" is vital, engaging with the MAP CoP has helped members to hone their skills in summarizing, writing, presenting, facilitating, and networking. Many have linked involvement in MAP activities to their professional registration with CILIP: the Library and Information Association[27] as a result of the skills and knowledge acquired.

Looking forward, the MAP CoP hopes to expand, growing and extending its reach to engage more library professionals from across the United Kingdom. Content for the MAP Toolkit will continue to be developed in response to feedback from the wider health sciences library community. Most of all, the aim is to empower library professionals, enabling them to articulate the impact of their work to senior leaders within their organizations, in a confident and powerful way.

REFERENCES

1. MAP Toolkit. Manchester: MAP Community of Practice; 2017. c2008–2017. Available from: https://maptoolkit.wordpress.com/.
2. Health and Social Care Act 2012. 2017. Available from: http://www.legislation.gov.uk/ukpga/2012/7/contents.
3. *Sustainability and Transformation Partnerships (STPs)*. London: NHS England; 2017. Available from: https://www.england.nhs.uk/stps/.
4. NHS Health Education England. *Knowledge for Healthcare: A Development Framework*. London: NHS Health Education England; December 2014. Available from: https://hee.nhs.uk/sites/default/files/documents/Knowledge%20for%20healthcare%20-%20a%20development%20framework.pdf.
5. Health Education England. *Learning Development Agreement*. London: Health Education England; 2015, 145 pages.
6. Pratchett T, Anderson L. *Smoke Signals from the 'Big Smoke': Aligning and Evaluating Health Libraries and Sharing Best Practice*. LIHHNK Up; March 30, 2009. Available from: http://www.lihnn.nhs.uk/images/Documents/LIHNN/LIHNNK-Up/LU_30_March2009.pdf.
7. Professor the Lord Darzi of Denham KBE. *High Quality Care for All: NHS Next Stage Review Final Report – Summary*. London: Department of Health; 2008. Available from: http://webarchive.nationalarchives.gov.uk/20130105061317/http://www.dh.gov.uk/prod_consum_dh/groups/dh_digitalassets/@dh/@en/documents/digitalasset/dh_085826.pdf.

8. Hill P. *Report of a National Review of NHS Health Library Services in England: From Knowledge to Health in the 21st Century*. London: National Library for Health; 2017. Available from: http://citeseerx.ist.psu.edu/viewdoc/download?doi=10.1.1.462.9667&rep=rep1&type=pdf.
9. England NHS. *NHS Commissioning*. London: NHS England; 2018. Available from: https://www.england.nhs.uk/commissioning/.
10. *A Million Decisions Campaign*. London: NHS Health Education England; 2017. Available from: https://hee.nhs.uk/our-work/research-learning-innovation/healthcare-library-knowledge-services/million-decisions-campaign.
11. NHS Health Education England. *NHS Library and Knowledge Services in England Policy*. London: NHS Health Education England; October 2016. Availabe from: https://hee.nhs.uk/sites/default/files/documents/Knowledge%20for%20Healthcare%20Policy%20Statement%20Nov%202016.pdf.
12. Al-Hawamdeh S. *Knowledge Management*. Oxford: Chandos Publishing; 2003.
13. *Health Libraries Group Newsletter*. London: CILIP; 2018. Available from: https://archive.cilip.org.uk/health-libraries-group/newsletter.
14. Cohen A. Libraries, knowledge management, and communities of practice. *Inf Outlook*. 2006;10(1):34–37.
15. *Library and Information Health Network NW (LIHNN)*. Wigan: LIHNN; 2017. Available from: http://www.lihnn.nhs.uk/index.php/lihnn/about-lihnn.
16. *Revalidation: Your Step by Step Guide through the Process*. London: Nursing Midwifery Council; 2018. Available from: http://revalidation.nmc.org.uk/.
17. *Revalidation for Nurses and Midwives*. Manchester: MAP Community of Practice; 2015. Available from: https://maptoolkit.wordpress.com/2015/10/16/revalidation-for-nurses-and-midwives/.
18. *Archived Content*. Manchester: MAP Community of Practice; 2017. Available from: https://maptoolkit.wordpress.com/projectmanagement/archived-drivers/.
19. Health Education England. *Knowledge Management Stories*. London: Health Education England; 2017. Available from: http://kfh.libraryservices.nhs.uk/knowledge-management/knowledge-management-story/.
20. *Hot Topic: Accountable Care Organisations*. Manchester: MAP Community of Practice; 2017. Available from: https://maptoolkit.wordpress.com/2017/05/09/hot-topic-accountable-care-organisations/.
21. Health Education England. *Knowledge for Healthcare (Blog)*. London: Health Education England; 2017. Available from: http://kfh.libraryservices.nhs.uk/.
22. Brettle A, Maden-Jenkins M, Anderson L, et al. Evaluating clinical librarian services: a systematic review. *Health Info Libr J*. 2010;28(1):3–22. https://doi.org/10.1111/j.1471-1842.2010.00925.x.
23. Brettle A, Maden M, Payne C. The impact of clinical librarian services on patients and health care organisations. *Health Info Libr J*. 2016;33(2):100–120. https://doi.org/10.1111/hir.12136.
24. *Patient and Public Information Drivers*. London: Health Education England; 2018. Available from: http://kfh.libraryservices.nhs.uk/patient-and-public-information/making-the-case-ppi/patient-and-public-information-drivers/.
25. *Knowledge Management*. London: Health Education England; 2018. Available from: http://kfh.libraryservices.nhs.uk/knowledge-management/.
26. *Value and Impact Toolkit*. London: Health Education England; 2018. Available from: http://kfh.libraryservices.nhs.uk/value-and-impact-toolkit/.
27. *CILIP: The Library and Information Association*. London: CILIP; 2018. Available from: https://www.cilip.org.uk/.

CHAPTER 5

Open Collaboration: How Separate Library Systems Harmonized Their Support for Open Access Scholarship

Denise A. Smith[1], Olga Perkovic[2], Gabriela Mircea[2]
[1]Health Sciences Library, Faculty of Health Sciences, McMaster University, Hamilton, ON, Canada;
[2]University Library, McMaster University, Hamilton, ON, Canada

INTRODUCTION

The open access movement aims to democratize access to knowledge worldwide and make publicly funded research available to the public.[1] The Berlin Declaration on Open Access to Knowledge in the Sciences and Humanities establishes open access contributions as works that grant users:

> *free, irrevocable, worldwide, right of access to, and a license to copy, use, distribute, transmit and display the work publicly and to make and distribute derivative works, in any digital medium for any responsible purpose, subject to proper attribution of authorship.*[2]

The impact of open access publishing models is profound. Open access models significantly extend the reach of research by removing economic barriers.[1] The models simultaneously have the potential to increase author citation metrics by virtue of the fact that the article will have a wider audience.[3]

In 2008, the Canadian Institutes of Health Research (CIHR) adopted an open access publication policy requiring published research funded by CIHR to be made open access within 12 months of publication. In autumn of 2013, the Natural Sciences and Engineering Research Council of Canada (NSERC) together with the Social Sciences and Humanities Research Council of Canada (SSHRC) also announced their plan to adopt split infinitive an open access publication policy to be harmonized with CIHR's existing policy. The result was unveiled as the Tri-Agency Open Access Policy for Publications: a single unified open access publication policy for NSERC, SSHRC, and CIHR—Canada's leading federal

Strategic Collaborations in Health Sciences Libraries
ISBN 978-0-08-102258-0
https://doi.org/10.1016/B978-0-08-102258-0.00005-7
Copyright © 2019 Jean P. Shipman and M.J. Tooey. Published by Elsevier Limited. All rights reserved.

funding agencies for research.[4] This new policy requires articles accepted for publication resulting from research funded by any of these three agencies to be made openly available to the public within 12 months of the original publication date.[4]

The Tri-Agency Open Access Policy for Publications was a great stride toward change in the way information is produced and published in Canada. This change might be challenging for researchers unfamiliar with open access or the new policy and who are funded by one of these three agencies. There are several ways a researcher or scholar can make their work open access and as with any relationship, the one between the open access movement and traditional publishing models is complicated. Librarians have a role in helping those who, either through obligation or by preference, wish to make their work open access. Librarians can help researchers navigate the publication labyrinth while balancing author rights and legal obligations to publishers. When it was announced that this new policy would come into effect on May 1, 2015, McMaster University Libraries was listening.

This chapter describes a case at McMaster University in Ontario, Canada where, under the direction of administration, two separate library systems collaborated to assess the needs of faculty and researchers as related to the Tri-Agency Open Access Policy. The unique nature of this approach is discussed in addition to the details of the work involved, the outcomes of the project, and the impact of collaboration at McMaster University Libraries and at other libraries within Canada.

BACKGROUND

McMaster University is home to four libraries. Three of these libraries cover business, science and engineering, and social sciences and humanities and are referred to as the University Library (UL). The UL operates under the direction of the university librarian. The Health Sciences Library (HSL) operates separately from the UL. It has its own director and is part of the Faculty of Health Sciences. Although all four libraries have different collections and serve different academic disciplines, both systems foster and support a culture of research at the university. In recent years, the university librarian and the director of the HSL have nurtured collaboration through ongoing discussions about how the libraries' can leverage their organizational strengths to meet common goals. One outcome of these discussions was the formation of the Open Access Working Group (OAWG).

DIRECTION

When the HSL and the UL formed the OAWG, the first goal was to synchronize two preexisting individual web pages hosted on the UL and HSL websites regarding the open access publishing model. In recognition of the duplication of effort involved in updating and maintaining two separate web pages, the OAWG received a directive from the university librarian and associate university librarians of the UL to curate and synchronize the content from both web pages into a single user-friendly web page. The OAWG also received a second directive to create an interactive tool to assist researchers and faculty in navigating the requirements of the Tri-Agency Open Access Publication Policy for Publications. Third, the OAWG was asked to develop and host an online video to briefly describe the new policy and its implications for researchers and faculty members.[5]

OAWG COMPOSITION AND ROLES

The OAWG was composed of six members:

1. A learning support coordinator (UL)
2. A research and advanced studies librarian (UL)
3. An education liaison librarian (HSL)
4. A student media and computing manager (UL)
5. A digital repository librarian (UL)
6. A public relations coordinator (UL)

The role of the UL learning support coordinator was to make the web page an accessible online resource for all users. This coordinator ensured that the content and design of the web page promoted inclusivity through compliance with the Accessibility for Ontarians with Disabilities Act (AODA),[6] the governing legislation for accessibility in Ontario, Canada.

The UL research and advanced studies librarian provided expertise in scholarly publishing, the open access publication model, and new or emerging trends in scholarly publishing. These knowledge and skills were valuable assets for the selection of accurate and appropriate content to include in the web page.

The HSL education liaison librarian took on several roles. First, the OAWG relied on this librarian's expertise in publication requirements for health research, as the CIHR had used an open access policy since 2008. The HSL education liaison librarian was able to provide insights into when the CIHR open access policy would be applicable and when the new

Tri-Agency Policy would trump the requirements of CIHR. This librarian made significant contributions to the drafting of content for the interactive tool and led the decision-making process regarding the inclusion or exclusion of content from the HSL open access web page.

The UL student media and computing manager, who was in charge of all staff and public computing for the UL, constructed the interactive tool and the online video. The UL digital repository librarian, who managed the technical infrastructure for the institutional repository, journal publishing, and digital preservation services, applied web development skills to design the new combined web page with a sharp focus on user experience.

Finally, the UL public relations coordinator, a split position between UL and the University Advancement Office, translated the OAWG members' expertise-specific jargon into language appropriate for all audiences. The UL public relations coordinator advised on the composition of a script for the animated video and also had significant input on the production of text content for the web page and interactive tool. This was fundamental in making the project outcomes easily digested by the intended users.

The composition of this cross-functional team fostered a culture of collaboration between the UL and the HSL. It presented an opportunity to challenge the existing paradigm that libraries at McMaster serve different types of user groups, often working alongside one another but not necessarily with each other. The OAWG was able to leverage the skills of all types of library workers to generate web content about open access benefitting the whole research community at McMaster University.

TIMELINE

The directive from the administrators of the UL and the HSL to form the OAWG came in early March 2015, shortly after the announcement of the new Tri-Agency Open Access Policy on Publications with its effective date of May 1, 2015. Tasked with completing the charge before the policy became effective, the timeline for the OAWG's work was tight. With limited time to contribute to the task, the OAWG met regularly and adopted the use of Google Drive, allowing each member to work independently between meetings. This "divide and conquer" approach was instrumental in the group completing the work within only 2 months.

OUTCOMES

The work of the OAWG had three primary outcomes presented on a single web page called Open Access, McMaster University Libraries.[7] The first, the *Guide to Open Access*, curated, combined, and synchronized all pre-existing textual content from both the HSL and the UL open access web pages into a single, accordion-style, drop-down question and answer menu. The second outcome, an animated video, provided a brief overview of the new Tri-Agency policy and the impact on government-funded faculty and researchers. The third outcome of the OAWG's work was an online interactive tool. This tool was designed to provide researchers and faculty with a custom list of action items to faciltate compliance with the Tri-Agency Policy.

Implementing these three outcomes into the design of the new web page required consideration of several key functional points. The OAWG sought to optimize the flow between the three different types of content. It was important to balance the textual content in the *Guide to Open Access* with the interactive tool and the video so users could easily navigate the content on the web page.

Guide to Open Access

The first deliverable for the OAWG was to synthesize the content from the existing web pages maintained separately by the HSL and the UL into a single web page to be used by researchers and faculty across all disciplines.

The OAWG established that all the existing information could fit elegantly into a single web page through the implementation of concise language and a collapsible accordion-style menu (see Fig. 5.1). This approach allowed users to toggle between hiding and showing a large amount of content. The OAWG worked zealously to combine and improve the textual content from existing resources into what became the *Guide to Open Access*. The OAWG organized the content into four main categories independent of each other and revised the messaging under the guidance of the UL public relations coordinator.

Animated Video

The second deliverable for the group was a short, animated video providing a pithy introduction to the new Tri-Agency Policy and explaining its impact on researchers and faculty at McMaster University.[8] Participation in the creation of a video was a new experience for most of the OAWG members.

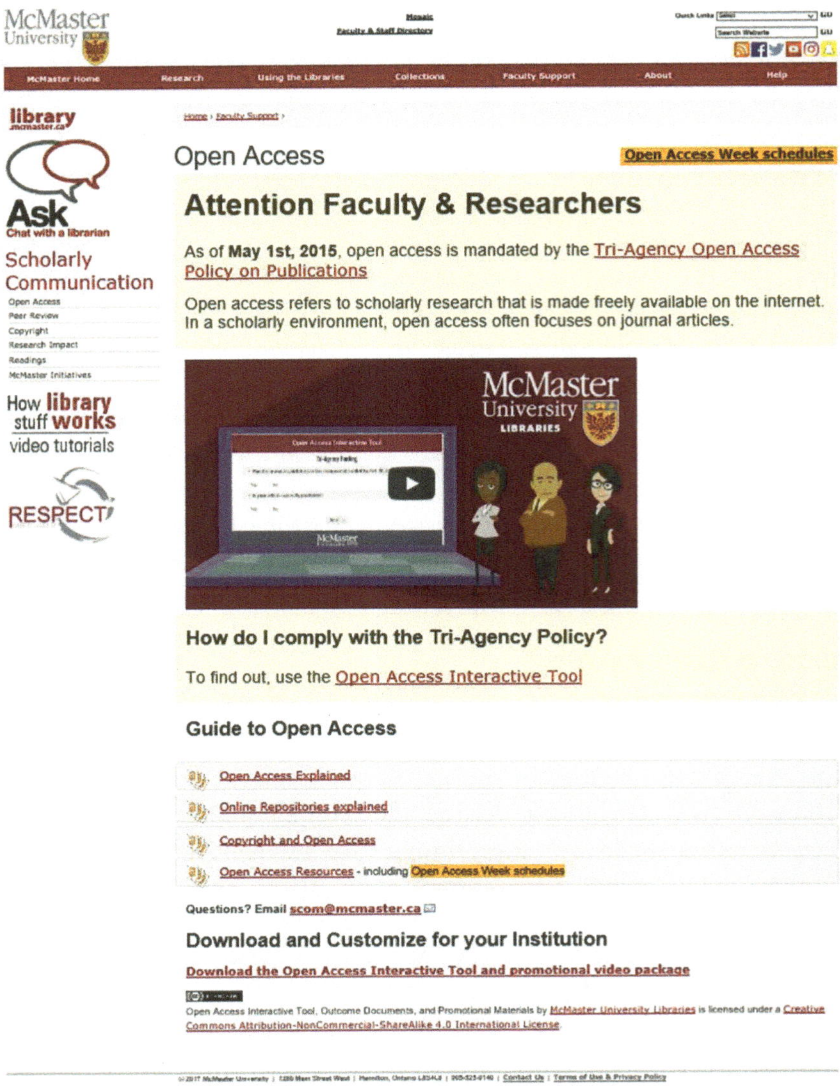

Figure 5.1 Open access landing page, featuring the Guide to Open Access.

The OAWG worked together to condense the policy from three pages of text into a 60-s script. Although this seemed simple at first glance, there were a few components that had to come together for the OAWG to be successful with this outcome. The script needed to communicate the essentials without sounding condescending. The OAWG paid attention to the tone and language of the script. With the significant reduction from three pages of text to a 60 s narration, it was important to be as clear as possible about the publishing requirements for publicly funded research.

Another element of building the video was the selection of a professional voice-over for narration. The OAWG used Voices.com, an online marketplace of over 200,000 voice actors.[9] This resource allowed the OAWG to collect bids from voice actors. The UL student media and computing manager curated an initial short list of candidates who received an early version of the video script. Each candidate submitted a recording of the script to the OAWG. The team listened to each recording and, by consensus, hired a voice actor whose voice was energetic, particularly clear, and not too casual.

The final element involved creating animated characters and moving graphics into the video. This was undertaken by the student media and computing manager. The process prompted a thorough negotiation process before the OAWG settled on the final video components. The OAWG combined its collective expertise to ensure the video was accessible and in compliance with the AODA. The OAWG also ensured that the animated characters were an inclusive representation of the body of faculty and researchers at McMaster University.

Interactive Tool

The development of the online interactive tool, linked from Open Access, McMaster University Libraries (http://library.mcmaster.ca/scholarly-communication/open-access) was the most labor-intensive of the three project outcomes. In addition to developing a tool that placed learning about the new open access policy in the hands of the user, the OAWG wanted to produce a tool that was easy to use and met the needs of the target audience. The OAWG relied heavily on rapid prototyping to see and understand the overall look and feel of the tool.

Two OAWG members with technical expertise were responsible for the evaluation of potential software to create the interactive tool. They assessed potential software for its compatibility with the OAWG's goals, including how well it met the requirements set by the rest of the OAWG, such as degree of interactivity or branching logic. After the software analysis was conducted and presented, it was agreed that LimeSurvey, a professional, open-source online tool for building surveys,[10] was the most appropriate software to use to construct the interactive tool. LimeSurvey was used in combination with the collaborative word processing cloud service, Google Docs.

The first step to develop the interactive tool involved mapping a thorough workflow for each possible scenario a researcher or faculty member might experience in relation to the Tri-Agency policy and the publication of their research.

While the two technical experts constructed the tool in LimeSurvey, shown in Fig. 5.2, the other OAWG members simultaneously drafted one-page summaries for each possible scenario in Google Docs. The summaries, shown in Fig. 5.3, outlined how the new policy impacted funded research and suggested next steps the user could take to comply with the new policy. These were produced as dynamic PDF documents, allowing any OAWG member to update content periodically and consequently autoupdate the downloadable web page summary document.

It was a significant challenge to find the right balance within the interactive tool. The tool was intended to be intuitive, not overly complicated, clean, accessible, and provide a seamless connection between the individual scenarios and the steps users needed to take to comply with the Tri-Agency policy. To find this balance, the public relations coordinator helped to ensure that the language used throughout the tool translated into something meaningful to users of varying research or academic disciplines.

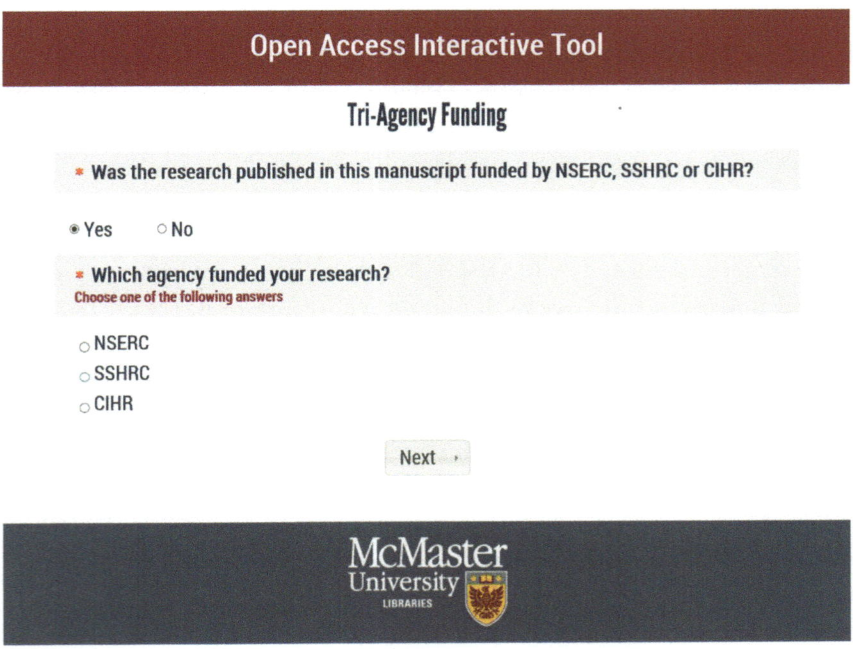

Figure 5.2 Screenshot of the interactive tool.

YOUR NEXT STEPS TO OPEN ACCESS...

You indicated that you received funding from NSERC or SSHRC on or after May 1, 2015, so the Tri-Agency Open Access Policy applies to the situation you specified. Your research is published, but not in an open access journal or in a journal that will make your article open access with 12 months of publication.

To meet the requirements of the Tri-Agency Policy, deposit your manuscript into an online repository.

Next Steps:

1. Consult SHERPA/RoMEO, a database of publishers' policies regarding the self-archiving of journal articles on the web or online repositories. You may have the right to include some, but not all, versions of your article (e.g. pre-print, post-print, or published version)
2. Contact your publisher to confirm your copyright permissions.
3. Deposit your manuscript into an online repository:
   a. MacSphere: McMaster's Institutional Repository
      i. Log-in to MacSphere with your MAC ID and password and submit your article to the collection that corresponds with your department
   b. Search or browse a list of subject-based repositories using *Open*DOAR: Directory of Open Access Repositories

Important Links:

- SHERPA/RoMEO: http://www.sherpa.ac.uk/romeo/
- MacSphere: https://macsphere.mcmaster.ca/
- *Open*DOAR: http://opendoar.org/index.html

Questions?

- Email scom@mcmaster.ca
- See the Guide to Open Access

Figure 5.3 Interactive tool downloadable document.

USAGE AND FEEDBACK

The OAWG produced a web page that delivered a package of three online resources for faculty and researchers at McMaster University. The OAWG's thoughtful and creative efforts resulted in a user-friendly, thorough, and well-prepared information resource about the Tri-Agency Open Access Policy on Publications and implications for publication of government-funded research. The impact of the outcomes of this work has been measurable. Since it was launched, the interactive tool has been used regularly. As of February 2018, it had more than 2200 uses. These usage statistics represent all uses, including those of library staff who tested the tool. As a result of the short timeline of the project, the OAWG launched the web page with limited user testing of all three outcomes.

In the context of soliciting feedback for the purpose of improving the tool, the OAWG included a very brief, but optional, feedback form on the results pages of the interactive tool. The form was completed by a few users soon after the launch of the tool, and minor revisions were made to the tool as a result. For example, access to the tool was changed from a pop-up window to a new browser tab to allow the user to scroll through the questions. The form remained in the tool for approximately 1 year, after which time, it was removed as few users had completed the form to describe their experience. It was assumed the tool successfully provided users with the information they sought or more comments would have been submitted. No formal analysis of the minimum data from the user feedback form was completed.

DISCUSSION

The most impressive accomplishment of the OAWG is that the project contributed to efforts at the administrative level to foster a culture of collaboration between librarians and library staff from the two library systems. In the initial invitation to participate in the OAWG, the UL Leadership Group and the director of the HSL also asked OAWG members to complete a second distinct piece of work in a short time frame.[5] In addition to the OAWG's work to build a web page supporting open access scholarship at the University, the second request asked for brief recommendations regarding areas and strategies for the UL and the HSL to work together on additional issues related to open access. The document produced in response to this request focused on one recommendation, the creation of a standing Open Access Committee to include representation from both library systems.

The Open Access Committee members would collaborate on open access education and initiatives across campus. In addition to working on events for the annual International Open Access Week event, Committee members would identify smaller projects and invite other library staff to join, as needed. Committee members would maintain the Open Access web page to ensure information remained current and accurate. This formal committee had not yet been formed at the time of publication; however, an OAWG with membership from the UL and the HSL continued to meet each fall term to coordinate and plan Open Access Week events. Two librarians, one from each library system, continued to collaborate on open access advocacy and event planning on the university campus.

OAWG members disseminated the work already accomplished. Some members of the OAWG proposed and prepared a presentation for the Ontario Library Association's 2016 annual conference.[11] The presentation was well attended prompting a series of questions from library administrators and other librarians in attendance.

OAWG members went on to collaborate on other projects. The HSL education liaison librarian reached out to the UL to combine efforts to host a special event on Wikipedia and health. Each year, a planning committee is formed to organize events for International Open Access Week. HSL librarian representatives have joined UL librarians in offering and jointly promoting sessions, presentations, and other activities. The HSL education liaison librarian and the UL research and advanced studies librarian jointly investigated the movement toward Open Educational Resources (OER) in Canadian colleges and universities. As members of McMaster University's OER working group, they have participated in, or attended, various OER initiatives, events, and presentations locally and provincially.

The OAWG's work also contributed to the movement toward collaboration, not just between the HSL and the UL but also with librarians in other institutions across Canada. The open access web page, video, and interactive tool were launched during a national meeting of university librarians and other leaders in Canadian libraries. This meeting provided an opportunity for the McMaster University Librarian to promote the launch of the page and related resource tools. As a result, librarians from other institutions and provinces have contacted the OAWG members about sharing the source files for the video and interactive tool in particular. The interactive tool and animated video were packaged without McMaster University branding under a Creative Commons Attribution-NonCommercial-ShareAlike 4.0 International License, meaning the outcomes of the OAWG's work were made available for adaptation and reuse by other institutions.[12]

Crucial to the OAWG's success was each member's ability and willingness to adopt new perspectives, adapt to differing skill sets and expertise, and trust in each other's expertise. This attitude encouraged open communication among the OAWG members. Each member provided comments and asked questions, especially about content outside their typical domain. This work provided a tremendous opportunity for learning. It lent the OAWG an ability to uncover solutions to challenges not easily seen by OAWG members who were more familiar with the context of the problem. For example, the UL public relations coordinator swayed the librarians on the OAWG away from the use of library-specific jargon when the script for the animated video was drafted. The UL public relations coordinator knew little about open access publishing and asked extremely valuable questions compelling the librarians to think more broadly about the audience and the appropriate language needed for the animated video.

For this project to succeed within the tight timeline, library administrative support was required. With the support of their supervisors, OAWG members set aside other work responsibilities to prioritize their commitment to this project. OAWG meetings took place once or twice per week and email communication was essential between meetings. The work remained a consistent priority until the web page and the supporting resources were launched. The OAWG did not anticipate the immediate interest it received from other libraries to reuse the package of customizable tools. When this occurred, some of the OAWG members continued to give this work top priority.

CONCLUSION

The introduction of the Tri-Agency Open Access Policy on Publications compelled the two separate library systems at McMaster University to approach this change as an opportunity for collaboration between the HSL and the UL. With the direction and support of administration from both Libraries, the two systems collaborated to assess the needs of faculty and researchers in all departments.

The outcomes of this work were built into a single web page synchronizing material previously existing on two distinct library web sites. The resulting accordion-style online guide, animated video, and the interactive tool were the products of a cross-functional and collaborative team where each member contributed unique expertise, allowing a holistic approach to this project. The OAWG's work attracted attention from other libraries in Canada and prompted the OAWG to take collaboration one-step further by packaging the materials without McMaster University branding a the Creative Commons License.

This work also encouraged librarians and library staff from the two library systems to engage in collaboration on other topics without prompts from the UL or the director of the HSL. For example, some OAWG members presented their work at a conference. Other OAWG members submitted a proposal to the UL to establish an on-going Open Access Committee including membership from both library systems. These librarians continued to collaborate on open access work and new initiatives addressing common emerging trends in academic and health sciences librarianship, such as the OER movement and conversations around the destigmatization of Wikipedia.

Looking ahead, both library systems can only benefit from further collaboration with each other. By leveraging their strengths, the two systems present students, faculty, researchers, and the non-McMaster community with a united approach to fostering excellence in education and research.

REFERENCES

1. Yiotis K, 22058 *The Open Access Initiative: A New Paradigm for Scholarly Communications. Inf Technol Libr.* 2018;24(4):157−162. https://doi.org/10.6017/ital.v24i4.3378.
2. *Berlin Declaration*; 2018. Available from: https://openaccess.mpg.de/Berlin-Declaration.
3. Tennant JP, Waldner F, Jacques DC, Masuzzo P, Collister LB, Hartgerink CHJ. The academic, economic and societal impacts of open access: an evidence-based review. *F1000Res.* September 21, 2016;5:632.
4. Government of Canada. *Tri-Agency Open Access Policy on Publications*; 2018. Available from: Science.gc.ca. http://www.science.gc.ca/eic/site/063.nsf/eng/h_F6765465.html?Open Document.
5. Lewis V. *Open Access - Invitation to Participate in Working Group.* Message to: Olga Perkovic, Leeane Romane, Denise Smith. February 24, 2015 [2 paragraphs].
6. Ontario G. *Of. Accessibility for Ontarians with Disabilities Act, 2005, S.O. 2005, c. 11 English View*; 2014. Ontario, Ca. Available from: https://www.ontario.ca/laws/view.
7. McMaster University Libraries. *Open Access.* Hamilton, Ontario, Canada: McMaster University Library; 2008. Available from: http://library.mcmaster.ca/scholarly-communi cation/open-access.
8. McMaster Libraries. *Open Access - McMaster Libraries*; 2018. Available from: https:// www.youtube.com/watch?v=K-iEIibyQKs.
9. Administrator. *Welcome to the #1 Marketplace for Voice over Talent*; 2018. Available from: Voices.com. https://www.voices.com.
10. *LimeSurvey: The Online Survey Tool - Open Source Surveys*; 2018. Available from: https:// www.limesurvey.org/.
11. Perkovic O, Romane L, Smith D. *Open Access Scholarship in the Library Lab: Generating Interactive Online Resources for Faculty and Researchers*; 2016. Available from: https:// macsphere.mcmaster.ca/handle/11375/19207.
12. *Creative Commons — Attribution-Noncommercial-ShareAlike 4.0 International — CC BY-NC-SA 4.0*; 2018. Available from: https://creativecommons.org/licenses/by-nc-sa/4. 0/.

CHAPTER 6

Bringing the Evidence to the Table: Librarians Partner With Performance Improvement for High-Quality, Safe, and Cost-Effective Patient Care

Megan von Isenburg[1], Jamie Conklin[2], Leila Ledbetter[1], Beverly Murphy[1], Megan Van Noord[1]
[1]Medical Center Library & Archives, Duke University, Durham, NC, United States; [2]Health Sciences Library, University of North Carolina at Chapel Hill, Chapel Hill, NC, United States

INTRODUCTION: THE CHANGING ENVIRONMENT OF HEALTH CARE

The health-care environment is changing. It is all over the news, and anybody who works in health care or even seeks a doctor for their own care recognizes it. Reports state that the US health-care system is the most costly in the world, accounting for almost 18% of the gross domestic product as of 2015, and estimates indicate continual growth as a result of an aging population, increased longevity, and prevalence of chronic health problems.[1] Hospital expenditure resources show that costs of procedures vary widely from state to state, or even from hospital to hospital. The days are gone when hospitals and health-care centers just pay what procedures cost and rely on hiring the best health-care professionals to make the best decisions on how to treat their patients. In response to rising costs and increased pressure on health-care systems to provide better and more efficient care, there is now a push toward what is frequently called Care Redesign, a process of quality improvement within health-care systems.

LITERATURE REVIEW

The quality improvement movement in health care began in the late 1980s and early 1990s with Berwick's call for continuous improvement[2] and the development of the Institute for Healthcare Improvement (IHI) aimed at

Strategic Collaborations in Health Sciences Libraries
ISBN 978-0-08-102258-0
https://doi.org/10.1016/B978-0-08-102258-0.00006-9
Copyright © 2019 Jean P. Shipman and M.J. Tooey. Published by Elsevier Limited. All rights reserved.

reducing errors, waste, delay, and costs within health care.[3] In 2007 the IHI introduced the Triple Aim, an initiative to achieve three goals: improve the care experience, improve the health of populations, and reduce the per capita costs of health care.[4] The design concept for achieving these goals include five components—a focus on families and individuals, the redesign of primary care services, management of population health, a platform for cost control, and system integration.

An early definition of Care Redesign expands the role of primary care to include a team of clinicians rather than a single physician and involves long-term relationships between patients and care teams.[5] The expanded view also invites patients to take an active role in their care coordination and in using personalized health records and improved scheduling options. In addition, there is an emphasis on connecting patients to community resources, which opens the possibility for librarians to take a more active role in providing health-related information.

Examples of Care Redesign processes have made their way into the literature with authors describing how they have been able to optimize costs, increase patient satisfaction, and reduce variation. For example, both the Duke University Health System and the University of Colorado Hospital redesigned care for congestive heart failure patients. Through a Heart@home initiative and Hospital to Home program aimed at reducing patient readmissions, the health-care centers created standardized post-discharge protocols including one outpatient follow-up visit within a week of discharge.[6] The University of Wisconsin School of Medicine and Public Health redesigned primary care and focused on reducing variation by standardizing the patient visit process from preplanning to postvisit and by introducing tools and procedures to make form completions and medication renewals more streamlined and consistent.[7]

Care Redesign benefits from the use of evidence within the medical literature and often centers on best practices and practice guidelines. For example, the redesign of care for radical cystectomy patients may include evidence regarding patient education, nutrition, care coordination, anesthesia, enhanced recovery protocols, pain management, and more.[8] This reliance on evidence provides the perfect opportunity for librarian involvement. To date, the librarian's role has been alluded to but not directly highlighted in the literature. For example, the colorectal surgery Care Redesign project at Vanderbilt included a literature search attributed to key stakeholders and led to the addition of a postoperative lidocaine infusion supported by a published systematic review. It is possible the key stakeholders involved were librarians, but this was not explicitly stated.[9]

In fact, the librarian's role in the broader quality improvement literature has not been robust or well documented. One study describes a librarian's participation with the Responsive Innovation Evidence Review, a quality improvement initiative with the Veterans Affairs and the Southern California Evidence-Based Practice Center. The librarian developed searches and wrote 13 reviews. Of these reviews, 50% of innovators found them to be "very useful" and 31% found them "probably useful."[10] Anecdotally, librarians are becoming more involved with quality improvement processes and have used search skills to drive performance improvement.[11,12]

Librarians have actively participated in Evidence-based Practice (EBP) on multiple levels, from teaching search and appraisal methods to conducting systematic searches for systematic reviews.[13,14] By providing health-care professionals with relevant information for more informed decision-making at the individual patient level, clinical librarian services have positively impacted patient care.[15] Likewise, there is certainly an opportunity for librarians to use their skills to positively impact Care Redesign and quality improvement processes occurring on a larger scale.

CARE REDESIGN AT DUKE

Duke Health employs over 30,000 people and consists of the School of Medicine, School of Nursing, the entire Duke University Health System (three hospitals and all the clinics), the Duke-NUS Medical School in Singapore, and the Private Diagnostic Clinic (Duke physicians practice). *US News and World Report* ranks Duke University Hospital as the number 17th medical center in the country.[16] Care Redesign is a key component in the "Transforming Our Future" strategic priority at Duke University Health System. The program began in the 2013 Fiscal Year to improve quality, experience, and efficiency across the care continuum for targeted patient conditions across all three Health System hospitals—Duke University Hospital, Duke Raleigh Hospital, and Duke Regional Hospital. The chief medical officer (CMO) for the Health System is the executive sponsor for the work, and his team identifies potential areas for redesign using a combination of metrics, including costs, clinician variability, and patient outcomes. Teams redesign care in specific areas over short time periods, often 16 weeks in duration. Target areas center around specific procedures, conditions, and hospitalwide processes. Example topics have included percutaneous coronary intervention, total knee replacement, colorectal surgery, pediatric asthma, adult septicemia, obstetric delivery, pediatric cardiothoracic surgery, renal failure, psychological and behavioral disorders, operating room utilization across the health system, and lung transplant.

All teams are interprofessional and can include physicians, nurses, social workers, librarians, pharmacists, financial analysts, information technology specialists, and others as needed. Staff from Performance Services lead the teams, though outside consultants played a role in designing and managing the process at one time. Performance Services direct Care Redesign teams through reviewing how care is currently delivered, assessing EBP, analyzing quality and efficiency data, and developing future processes to execute on opportunities.

LIBRARIAN ROLE IN CARE REDESIGN

The Medical Center Library serves the information needs of Duke Health and consists of approximately 25 staff members, 10 of whom are professional librarians. The Library uses a liaison model to organize most instruction and outreach activities to academic groups and hospital nursing. All librarians participate in research services by staffing virtual reference, while a smaller core of liaison librarians offer advanced services in systematic reviews and EBP instruction.

The Care Redesign partnership between the Health System and the Library resulted from the Library's role with teaching EBP. Librarians teach EBP in the School of Medicine, School of Nursing, Physician Assistant Program, and the Doctor of Physical Therapy program. In addition, librarians co-teach EBP with chief residents in internal medicine, pediatrics, and other residency programs and serve as faculty at a continuing medical education workshop on EBP. Librarians are therefore seen as experts in identifying evidence for clinical care decision-making. Accordingly, the librarian's primary function in the Care Redesign process and team role is to find and share the best evidence.

Performance Services establish Care Redesign teams and request a librarian's participation in each. Librarians are selected for teams based on availability and interest and are assigned before the launch of each new wave of Care Redesign. The librarian typically fulfills three types of requests within the scope of the project team:

1. Leading evidence: The research librarian identifies key governmental and society guidelines in the practice area and any published systematic reviews on the topic and provides them to the team lead before the team launches.
2. Best practices for focus areas: After the team has launched, the team lead conducts interviews with staff in the practice areas, such as social work, nutritional services, and nursing. These interviews and the leading evidence inform the selection of a set of core focus areas including such things as length of stay reduction, patient education, or medication management. The large team selects members to work on each focus area as a small group. The librarian then researches best practices in those focus areas. This typically involves identifying the best available evidence on these topics using the classic EBP hierarchy of evidence as a guide. After conducting topical searches, the librarian will frequently look through the results and select systematic reviews, randomized controlled trials, or large cohort studies to share with the small groups, concentrating on each focus area as they begin their work.
3. Deep dive research requests: Once the small groups begin working in their focus areas, questions often arise. Sometimes groups have background questions about specific diseases or conditions, which require selecting appropriate resources from textbooks and databases such as UpToDate. More often, groups have foreground questions, so librarians retrieve primary research from databases such as PubMed and preappraised literature from clinical practice guidelines, systematic reviews, and point of care tools like DynaMed Plus. Examples of foreground questions include "Can epidurals be given to women who test positive for cocaine?"; "What length of stay reductions can be expected from implementing the ABCDE bundle in the ICU?"; and "What are the benefits of a breast milk prep room in the NICU?" To facilitate the short timelines for these small groups, the research librarian seeks answers to the questions in a quick turnaround time, usually 24—48 hours. Information requests from small groups also include the name of a topic expert in case the librarian needs to consult about questions arising during the search. Whenever possible, librarians seek to provide an answer highlighted in a high-quality article or other information source.

In addition to filling these three types of requests, librarians participate in team meetings as often as possible. This allows them to hear questions that may not be articulated formally and to proactively provide research services without the team needing to make an official research request.

IMPACT OF CARE REDESIGN

From 2013 to 2017, Duke Health System implemented a total of 38 Care Redesign initiatives. These initiatives have led to reduced costs, more efficient workflows, better patient outcomes, and improved patient satisfaction. Team members, including librarians, dedicated time outside their normal work duties to define goals, access and evaluate evidence, brainstorm improvements to processes, and implement these process improvement initiatives. All these steps were completed with the patient in mind. One Care Redesign group began by mapping the entire patient process, beginning in the parking deck to imagine the patient experience from the point they arrive. Other teams focused on moving visits from specialists to other care providers, increasing consistency of care across Duke Health, and enhancing the electronic medical records.

Outcomes varied according to team focus. One team reduced the number of surgical trays providers could choose from, which has the potential to reduce both costs and provider variation. Another team changed the times of rounds to facilitate cross-team communication. Several teams produced updated and improved patient education materials. Almost all teams requested changes to workflows in Maestro Care, Duke's implementation of the Epic Electronic Health Record.

IMPACT OF LIBRARIANS' CONTRIBUTIONS

Librarians became involved in 2014 and have worked with 19 different teams, playing a critical role in identifying the best evidence and available information on implementation of best practices. Librarians have captured detailed statistics for 16 initiatives, logging over 160 requests and hand-selecting and delivering 1246 articles and 1463 citations (see Fig. 6.1). Librarians have spent over 272 hours searching, reviewing citations, and summarizing answers to questions (where relevant); this does not include time spent in meetings with teams (see Fig. 6.2).

The number of requests, articles, citations, and time expended varied widely by group, which reflects the individual and highly variable nature of each initiative. On average, each initiative generated 10 information requests, which resulted in the delivery of an average of 77 full-text articles and 121 citations. Variations seemed to relate more to group processes or goals rather than librarian characteristics or workflows. For example, the same librarian worked on both the initiative with the least amount and the

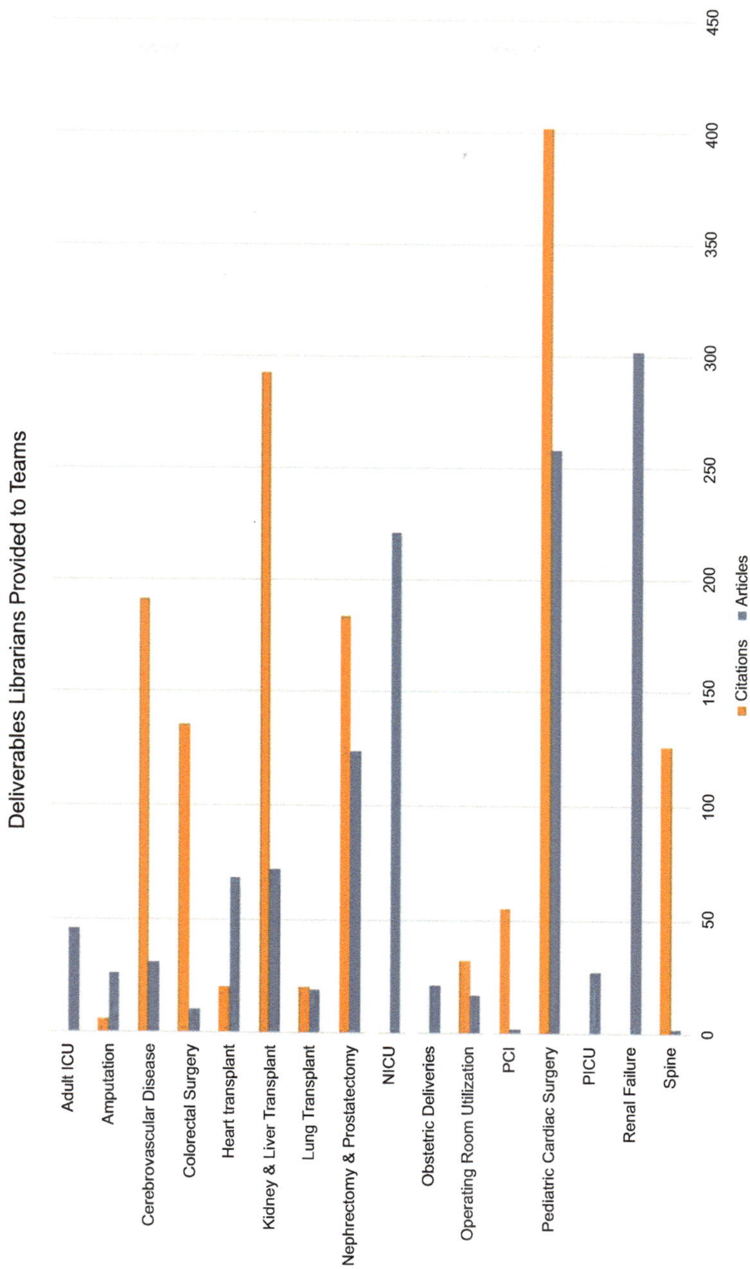

Figure 6.1 Numbers of citations and full-text articles provided to each team by librarians.

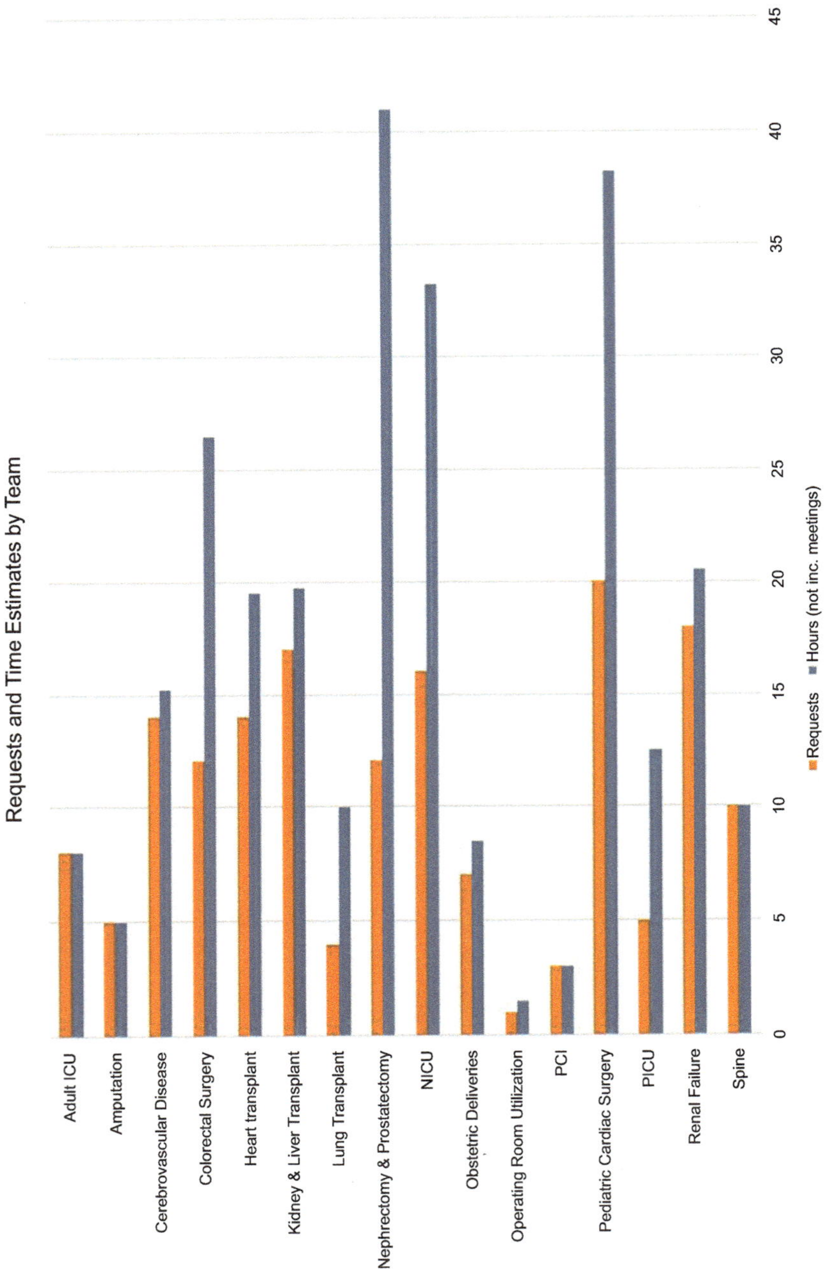

Figure 6.2 Numbers of requests and hours librarians spent answering research questions for each team.

initiative with the most amount of questions. In addition, most requests took an average of 1 hour per request, though for some initiatives this average was higher at 2 hours (Neonatal Intensive Care Unit (NICU), Pediatric Cardiac Surgery and Colorectal Surgery), 2 $^{1}/_{2}$ hours (Pediatric Intensive Care Unit (PICU) and Lung Transplant), and even 3 $^{1}/_{2}$ hours (Nephrectomy and Prostatectomy). This investment of time reflects the varying complexity of the initiative questions.

Librarians' contributions in the Care Redesign process have facilitated networking opportunities within the wider Health System. As librarians became integrated in Care Redesign teams, they raised awareness of Library resources and services by collaborating with health professionals in a wide array of disciplines with the common goal of supporting the larger Health System mission. This helped cement librarians' value in interdisciplinary research teams, led to improved satisfaction with Library services, and created additional opportunities to collaborate with administrators, researchers, and clinicians. For example, librarians have started conversations with the DUHS associate CMO for Patient Safety and Clinical Quality about a possible role for the Library in safety initiatives. Perhaps more importantly, it has given librarians a seat at the table with health system administrators.

IMPACT ON LIBRARIANS AND THE LIBRARY

The focus of academic health sciences librarians is primarily centered on supporting students, faculty, and researchers. Occasionally they are asked to find evidence relating to changes in procedures or to investigate something directly related to patient care. However, there is usually very little context for the question inside the overall patient care and hospital environment. Participating in Care Redesign teams provides a forest view of the health-care environment and issues the Health System is facing and the problems it is working to solve. Through Care Redesign participation, librarians better understand and engage in the workflows of the hospitals, providing a greater understanding of how clinicians and staff work together to problem-solve, all the while focusing heavily on the patient experience.

Working on interdisciplinary teams with clinicians helps librarians become better at being proactive in building partnership scenarios. They see the issues through a different lens and gain knowledge about specific topics by deep diving for information and distributing it to teams. Research and education librarians involved in the Care Redesign process have also found it helpful to incorporate these topics as examples when teaching EBP.

On a more personal level, it is rewarding to see the direct applicability of the work librarians do—finding high-quality evidence and seeing it put into practice on a larger scale. It is also gratifying to have team members better understand how the Library and Library staff can assist them with their questions. Librarians feel more connected with the Health System enterprise and more committed to the Library's mission. Additionally, Care Redesign participation aligns the Library's strategic goals to those of the Health System.

TIPS FOR CREATING PARTNERSHIPS

Across the Medical Center

Think Beyond Traditional User Groups

Hospital administration is often overlooked when establishing Library outreach or liaison services. Personnel in administration include data analysts, administrators, procurement officials, quality engineers, and finance analysts. Though they may be outside the traditional academic users around which libraries typically focus services, these individuals conduct research, seek the best evidence, and increasingly coordinate quality improvement work.

Other promising partners include patient education and quality improvement units. At Duke, two librarians serve on the Patient Education Governance Council and offer feedback on readability and health literacy of patient education materials. As another example, at Deaconess Hospital in Evansville, Indiana, the library manager trained with a team in Six Sigma, a quality improvement program aimed at eliminating process defects, and then applied her search skills to inform a quality improvement project.[17]

Invite Yourself to the Table

Outreach to new groups can have great impact, but how can librarians get a seat at the table? At some institutions, demonstrating the library's return on investment may be most effective. While it was not used with this group, the Cost Benefit and ROI Calculator for the National Network of Libraries of Medicine may be helpful.[18]

At Duke, two librarians "cold-called" Performance Services to offer a quick overview of Library resources and services to assist with new regulations and financial incentives regarding readmissions and other measures of quality. At the resulting meeting, it became clear Library resources were highly useful but rarely thought of in this business environment. Since the meeting, librarians have been asked back to offer training in PubMed searching and other resources to a growing group of performance services engineers who look at organizational change, cost, and quality.

Outreach to procurement has resulted in some interest, but fewer direct research requests. Librarians have participated in the review of procurement tools offering safety analysis and comparative effectiveness data on durable medical equipment. Librarians can offer expert guidance in identifying studies of effectiveness or harm and in triaging levels of evidence provided by industry for products.

Collect in New Areas

Libraries can also provide collections supporting hospital administration. The types of materials needed may fall outside typical academic medical journals. For example, the Performance Services group requested more journals in industrial engineering, which offer research and case studies in organizational change and efficiency—topics of great interest to improving health-care delivery.

Within Teams

Be an Advocate

Some of the challenges experienced in Care Redesign at Duke are not specific to the librarians' roles, but are instead more generalized obstacles to using and implementing the best available research evidence. Studies have consistently shown that providers often lack the time, skills, and access to resources to answer clinical questions.[19] Institutional culture and team dynamics can be barriers to EBP, particularly for providers who may fear disapproval from others on their team.[20,21] Even when institutional barriers are removed, completing the EBP cycle is challenging for many clinicians because the process itself creates ambiguity. For example, Ely and Osheroff[22] note there are challenges in articulating and refining an answerable question and uncertainty when assessing whether all the appropriate evidence has been found and the cycle is complete.

The Care Redesign experience reflects these challenges. Even though librarians had both the time and skills to find the evidence, members of the teams often lacked the time to review and analyze the provided evidence. Regular meetings with the medical director and program manager of Care Redesign have helped librarians to refine the process encouraging teams to "close the loop" on the evidence given to them. One idea was to create an evidence-tracking form requiring teams to note how their final plan relates to the found evidence.

Embed Yourself in Teams

Librarians may find it most useful to embed themselves within teams. By attending group and subgroup meetings, librarians are better able to listen for and discover information needs and to conduct reference interviews. For example, the librarian working with the lung transplant team was asked by the project manager to determine when patients should be given a certain swallowing study, but little evidence was available. Through a conversation with the nutrition team and physician, it became clear the underlying question was really about the risk of a specific adverse event. It was then possible to find a study reporting this event, so a decision could be made about the need for and timing of the swallowing study.

Attendance offers insight into the inner operations of the topic itself, thereby providing useful knowledge in retrieving relevant literature. It also saves time for team members as they do not have to draft emails to librarians afterward to forward questions. When physical attendance is not possible, librarians may be able to participate through online venues, such as Skype.

Assert Yourself and Promote Your Expertise

Realizing up-front, Care Redesign participants may not recognize the value of having a librarian on their teams, librarians should take time to introduce themselves and speak up during meetings when they see a potential information need. Librarians should use their expertise helping groups formulate questions, identifying potential useful information resources, and explaining study types and critical appraisal techniques. One example might be how to read forest plots when looking at a meta-analysis.

Lead Information Sharing and Access Efforts

Librarians can take an active role in helping Care Redesign teams determine the most efficient and practical way to share and preserve files and information sources. To do so, initiate conversations within groups about their preferences and be prepared to teach new technologies. For example, groups may prefer to use a cloud-based collaboration tool like Google Drive or Box. Others may prefer to rely on email or a citation manager, e.g., EndNote, when storing and reviewing articles. Librarians should ask group members what they prefer to receive—annotated bibliographies, citation lists, full-text articles, or other formats. Librarians should be prepared to talk about the advantages and disadvantages of chosen methods and be proactive in helping decide how to overcome potential information-sharing challenges. Librarians should lend their professional expertise so as not to be placed in an administrative assistant role.

Librarians should determine which information resources and collections available through local consortia and interlibrary loan programs can be leveraged in addition to robust local library collections. Librarians should recognize there may be resources that are locally unavailable, but could be helpful for literature searches. For example, Care Redesign librarians found it difficult to answer benchmarking questions requiring investigating standard operating procedures at other institutions because many do not share such information in published literature or through their web presences. Likewise, questions about proprietary information such as financials and resource procurement were challenging to answer as financial and benchmarking networks like Advisory Board[23] or the Vizient University Health System Consortium[24] are not licensed by the Library. Librarians should be open about these challenges and work with administrators to identify ways to either gain access to needed resources or to find other workarounds.

CONCLUSION

At the beginning of 2018, librarians at Duke have participated in Care Redesign teams for over 3 years and have found their contributions to be a gratifying and rare opportunity to see the direct application of their efforts. Though librarians answer research questions, it can take years for findings to be published and applied to patient care. With Care Redesign, librarians and Library users see the immediate value, as quality improvement projects move at a faster pace and lead to immediate changes to health system practices and policies.

Participating in Care Redesign teams demonstrates the value of librarians to administrators, project managers, and staff directly involved with patient care. It can lead to an expanded user base and offer a unique networking opportunity. Taking on this role also facilitates professional growth in health sciences librarianship.

REFERENCES

1. United States Center for Medicare & Medicaid Services. *National Health Expenditure Projections 2016-2025*. Baltimore, MD: Center for Medical & Medicaid Services; 2016. Available from: https://www.cms.gov/Research-Statistics-Data-and-Systems/Statistics-Trends-and-Reports/NationalHealthExpendData/Downloads/proj2016.pdf.
2. Berwick DM. Continuous improvement as an ideal in health care. *N Engl J Med*. 1989;320(1):53–56. https://doi.org/10.1056/nejm198901053200110. Epub 1989/01/05. PubMed PMID: 2909878.
3. Institute for Healthcare Improvement. *About Us: History*. Boston, MA: Institute for Healthcare Improvement; 2017. Available from: http://www.ihi.org/about/Pages/History.aspx.
4. Institute for Healthcare Improvement. *Initiatives: The IHI Triple Aim*. Boston, MA: Institute for Healthcare Improvement; 2017. Available from: http://www.ihi.org/Engage/Initiatives/TripleAim/Pages/default.aspx.
5. Berwick DM, Nolan TW, Whittington J. The triple aim: care, health, and cost. *Health Aff (Millwood)*. 2008;27(3):759–769. https://doi.org/10.1377/hlthaff.27.3.759. Epub 2008/05/14. PubMed PMID: 18474969.
6. George M, Bencic S, Bleiberg S, Alawa N, Sanghavi D. Case study: delivery and payment reform in congestive heart failure at two large academic centers. *Healthcare (Amst Neth)*. 2014;2(2):107–112. https://doi.org/10.1016/j.hjdsi.2014.04.001. Epub 2015/08/08. PubMed PMID: 26250378.
7. Koslov S, Trowbridge E, Kamnetz S, Kraft S, Grossman J, Pandhi N. Across the divide: "Primary care departments working together to redesign care to achieve the Triple Aim". *Healthcare (Amst Neth)*. 2016;4(3):200–206. https://doi.org/10.1016/j.hjdsi.2015.12.003. Epub 2016/09/18. PubMed PMID: 27637827; PubMed Central PMCID: PMCPmc5027069.
8. Matulewicz RS, Brennan J, Pruthi RS, Kundu SD, Gonzalez CM, Meeks JJ. Radical cystectomy perioperative care redesign. *Urology*. 2015;86(6):1076–1086. https://doi.org/10.1016/j.urology.2015.09.001. Epub 2015/09/19. PubMed PMID: 26383615.
9. McEvoy MD, Wanderer JP, King AB, et al. A perioperative consult service results in reduction in cost and length of stay for colorectal surgical patients: evidence from a healthcare redesign project. *Perioper Med (Lond Engl)*. 2016;5:3. https://doi.org/10.1186/s13741-016-0028-1. Epub 2016/02/09. PubMed PMID: 26855773; PubMed Central PMCID: PMCPmc4743367.
10. Danz MS, Hempel S, Lim YW, et al. Incorporating evidence review into quality improvement: meeting the needs of innovators. *BMJ Qual Saf*. 2013;22(11):931–939. https://doi.org/10.1136/bmjqs-2012-001722. Epub 2013/07/09. PubMed PMID: 23832925; PubMed Central PMCID: PMCPmc3812883.
11. Sollenberger JF, Holloway Jr RG. The evolving role and value of libraries and librarians in health care. *JAMA*. 2013;310(12):1231–1232. https://doi.org/10.1001/jama.2013.277050. Epub 2013/09/26. PubMed PMID: 24065006.
12. Marshall JG, Sollenberger J, Easterby-Gannett S, et al. The value of library and information services in patient care: results of a multisite study. *J Med Libr Assoc*. 2013;101(1):38–46. https://doi.org/10.3163/1536-5050.101.1.007. Epub 2013/02/19. PubMed PMID: 23418404; PubMed Central PMCID: PMCPmc3543128.
13. Rethlefsen ML, Farrell AM, Osterhaus Trzasko LC, Brigham TJ. Librarian co-authors correlated with higher quality reported search strategies in general internal medicine systematic reviews. *J Clin Epidemiol*. 2015;68(6):617–626. https://doi.org/10.1016/j.jclinepi.2014.11.025. Epub 2015/03/15. PubMed PMID: 25766056.

14. Swanberg SM, Dennison CC, Farrell A, et al. Instructional methods used by health sciences librarians to teach evidence-based practice (EBP): a systematic review. *J Med Libr Assoc.* 2016;104(3):197–208. https://doi.org/10.3163/1536-5050.104.3.004. Epub 2016/07/02. PubMed PMID: 27366120; PubMed Central PMCID: PMCPmc4915637.
15. Brettle A, Maden-Jenkins M, Anderson L, et al. Evaluating clinical librarian services: a systematic review. *Health Info Libr J.* 2011;28(1):3–22. https://doi.org/10.1111/j.1471-1842.2010.00925.x. Epub 2011/02/15. PubMed PMID: 21314890.
16. Health Duke. *Facts & Statistics 2017.* Durham, NC: Duke University; 2017, 2004–2017. Available from: https://corporate.dukehealth.org/who-we-are/facts-statistics.
17. Esparza JM. A librarian's experience with Six Sigma tools. *J Hosp Librariansh.* 2008;8(3):332–343. https://doi.org/10.1080/15323260802209500. PubMed PMID: 34592246.
18. National Network of Libraries of Medicine. *Cost Benefit and ROI Calculator.* Salt Lake City, UT: National Library of Medicine; 2017. Available from: https://nnlm.gov/mcr/professional-development/program-evaluation/cost-benefit-and-roi-calculator.
19. Jette DU, Bacon K, Batty C, et al. Evidence-based practice: beliefs, attitudes, knowledge, and behaviors of physical therapists. *Phys Ther.* 2003;83(9):786–805. PubMed PMID: 12940766.
20. Bhandari M, Montori V, Devereaux PJ, Dosanjh S, Sprague S, Guyatt GH. Challenges to the practice of evidence-based medicine during residents' surgical training: a qualitative study using grounded theory. *Acad Med.* 2003;78(11):1183–1190. Epub 2003/11/08. PubMed PMID: 14604884.
21. Green ML, Ruff TR. Why do residents fail to answer their clinical questions? A qualitative study of barriers to practicing evidence-based medicine. *Acad Med.* 2005;80(2):176–182. https://doi.org/10.1097/00001888-200502000-00016. PubMed PMID: 15671325.
22. Ely JW, Osheroff JA, Ebell MH, et al. Obstacles to answering doctors' questions about patient care with evidence: qualitative study. *BMJ.* 2002;324(7339):710. Epub 2002/03/23. PubMed PMID: 11909789; PubMed Central PMCID: PMCPmc99056.
23. Advisory Board. *About Us.* Washington, DC: Advisory Board; 2017. Available from: https://www.advisory.com/about-us.
24. Vizient. *About Us.* Irving, TX: Vizient; 2017. Available from: https://www.vizientinc.com/About-us.

CHAPTER 7

Successful Collaborations at the Local and National Level Build Teenagers' Skills to Advocate for Improved Health: Project SHARE

Alexa Mayo, M.J. Tooey
Health Sciences and Human Services Library, University of Maryland, Baltimore, Baltimore, MD, United States

BACKGROUND

In the spring of 2010, a team of faculty librarians from the Health Sciences and Human Services Library (HS/HSL) at the University of Maryland, Baltimore (UMB), successfully competed for a National Library of Medicine (NLM) Information Resource Grant to Reduce Health Disparities. The grant provided funds to support the HS/HSL's *Project SHARE: Student Health Advocates Redefining Empowerment* (2011–14) (G08LM011079), aimed at building high school students' skills to reduce health disparities at the personal, family, and community level. Academic health sciences librarians collaborated with partners at an urban high school to design the curriculum. Library initiatives to improve community health often involve showing community members how to access information or providing them with health information. Project SHARE expanded upon this approach by empowering people—in this case, teens—with health literacy and advocacy skills to advocate for improved health for themselves and for their communities within Baltimore.

According to *Healthy Baltimore 2020*, health disparities are a serious concern in the city, with data on major health indicators showing higher rates of chronic disease incidence and mortality than for Maryland or the United States.[1] The city has a mortality rate nearly 30% higher than the rest of the state and ranks last on key health outcomes compared with other jurisdictions in Maryland.[1] With more than one in three of Baltimore's children living below the federal poverty line, and more than 30% of Baltimore households earning less than $25,000 per year, income, poverty, and race have an enormous impact on health outcomes.[1] Neighborhood

Strategic Collaborations in Health Sciences Libraries
ISBN 978-0-08-102258-0
https://doi.org/10.1016/B978-0-08-102258-0.00007-0
Copyright © 2019 Jean P. Shipman and M.J. Tooey. Published by Elsevier Limited. All rights reserved.

disparities are revealed by the Baltimore City Health Department's *Neighborhood Health Profiles*, which shows a 16-year life-expectancy gap between residents of the city's Franklin Square community in Southwest Baltimore (68 years)[2] versus that of the wealthy North Baltimore/Guilford/Homeland neighborhoods (84 years).[3] It is within this setting that UMB applies its strengths to improve the health of neighboring communities.

INSTITUTIONAL FOUNDATION FOR COLLABORATION

University of Maryland, Baltimore

The composition of UMB is unique. In addition to the schools of Medicine, Dentistry, Nursing, and Pharmacy, there are the schools of Law and Social Work. These human services–oriented schools, combined with UMB's diverse population, academic strengths, and location within Baltimore, make it an ideal place not only for research but also for service partnerships in health care. Each of the UMB schools has significant involvement in community-based partnerships, programs, and projects, and UMB as a whole maintains the Office of Community Engagement, the Promise Heights Neighborhood Initiative, the Center for Minority Health Research, and the Ruth H. Young Center for Families and Children. UMB's students, faculty, and employees contribute more than two million hours of community service annually to citizens throughout Maryland.[4]

Strategic Plan

UMB formalizes its strong commitment to community engagement through its strategic plan. The plan identifies six key themes that contain a strategic objective and up to six strategic outcomes. The "Health, Justice, Social Impact" theme includes a commitment to deepen and expand local and global engagement to improve health. A strategic outcome within the theme is "the strong relationship with the Baltimore community in which UMB is viewed as a local resource and trusted partner by its residents and neighbors."[5] The strategic plan of HS/HSL aligns with that of UMB's. One of the goal of HS/HSL within the "Health, Justice, Social Impact" theme is to "advance health and well-being in our communities through support of innovative health information outreach projects."[6] In practice and on paper, the HS/HSL has a long-standing institutional commitment to health information outreach.

Health Sciences and Human Services Library

The HS/HSL was uniquely positioned to deliver on a project to reduce health disparities, drawing upon its strong team of faculty librarians, with expertise in health literacy and health information outreach, and in designing in-person and online training for health professionals and members of the community. The HS/HSL has provided liaison services to the university community for over 30 years. Faculty librarians within the Research, Education, and Outreach Department were experienced in collaborating with community partners to assess needs, design and deliver quality instruction, create support materials, and evaluate programs. The HS/HSL is also home to the National Network of Libraries of Medicine, Southeastern Atlantic Region (NNLM SEA), whose mission is to advance the progress of medicine and improve public health. This program provides US health professionals with equal access to biomedical information and improves public access to information, enabling consumers to make informed decisions about their health. This is accomplished by creating partnerships with regional libraries and professional and grassroots organizations. In FY16, over 5000 community members were reached through the HS/HSL and NNLM SEA's outreach services and programs.

In the years leading up to the SHARE Project, faculty librarians collaborated with diverse community groups within Baltimore and beyond. In 1995–96, a team at the HS/HSL worked with staff at community health centers to design and train community health workers and HIV-positive patients in locating AIDS information. The outreach team also collaborated with faith community nurses in Maryland to develop programming in locating quality health information. In 2007–08, the UMB School of Social Work's Community Outreach Service and the HS/HSL partnered to increase access to health information in underserved Baltimore neighborhoods. To understand the information needs of Marylanders, a team of faculty librarians conducted a statewide needs assessment by collaborating with a variety of stakeholders—staff at community-based organizations, teachers, unaffiliated health-care providers, and more. The HS/HSL also hosted Maryland Health Go Local (2005–06), an NLM-supported nationwide project linking health resources to local services throughout Maryland. In an innovative program outside of Maryland, the HS/HSL collaborated with UMB's School of Medicine and with international partners to develop services and programs at the University of Nairobi, College of Health Sciences Library.

These selected outreach programs and activities illustrate the breadth of the HS/HSL's expertise and commitment to engage with partners to improve health. It is with this history of community engagement and outreach experience that the HS/HSL collaborated with a West Baltimore high school, Vivien T. Thomas Medical Arts Academy (VTTMAA), to address health disparities through Project SHARE.

Vivien T. Thomas Medical Arts Academy

Project partner, VTTMAA, opened its doors in September 2004 as a community high school with an emphasis on preparing students to enter the fields of science, mathematics, and health-care professions. Almost all students (92%) are African American and most have low income.[7] Located only blocks from UMB, the high school presented an ideal opportunity for collaboration because its students were underserved, and its mission was to expose students to and prepare them for careers in health sciences.

The groundwork for the HS/HSL's successful collaboration with VTTMAA began years before Project SHARE was envisioned. In 2008, the UMB director of strategic initiatives and community partnerships approached the VTTMAA to discuss forming a partnership that would provide students with learning opportunities. The partnership blossomed into UMB's Summer Biomedical Internship Program. Through this program, up to 25 students interested in research were placed in laboratories for a summer internship experience. UMB's Institute for Genome Sciences offered five VTTMAA students a weeklong summer Science, Technology, Engineering, and Math (STEM) program, providing a hands-on experience in isolating DNA. In addition to working with VTTMAA to design learning experiences for students, the UMB director of strategic initiatives and community partnerships has been an active member of the VTTMAA's School and Family Council. The Council provides a forum for representative groups of school stakeholders, such as school faculty, staff, students, parents, and community members, to come together around a range of important school decisions.

With a relationship already in place, an HS/HSL faculty librarian reached out to the principal of VTTMAA to suggest the idea of a project to help develop health literacy and advocacy skills in VTTMAA students. This collaboration was only possible because a solid, trusting relationship between the institutions was already in place.

A TEAM ENVISIONS THE PROJECT

To begin outlining the concept for the project, the Project SHARE Team (the Team)—consisting of the School of Medicine liaison, outreach librarian, head of the liaison services, associate director of services, and the HS/HSL executive director—met over a course of several weeks to brainstorm innovative approaches to reducing health disparities. The Team decided to focus the project on building health advocacy skills in teens, with an emphasis on experiential learning.

Work began with researching peer-to-peer student programs, successful health advocacy programs, and the barriers to achieving health equity. The Team conducted a comprehensive review of the literature and reached out to project managers of teen health information projects by phone to discuss the successes and challenges involved in these programs. Early in the development of the vision for the project, a Team member contacted the principal and the guidance counselor at VTTMAA to gauge interest in the project. A member of the Team also contacted faculty and staff at UMB who had worked with VTTMAA students and faculty to identify successful partnership strategies and barriers to success.

The Team worked together to draft and submit the National Institutes of Health grant application. In its final conception, the project had three main aims: (1) empower high school students as community health advocates; (2) promote improved health in Baltimore neighborhoods; and (3) develop a replicable student health advocacy program. With notification of funding, Project SHARE began in March 2011.

PROJECT SHARE YEARS ONE AND TWO

Prior to the end of the 2010–11 school year, the Team, with the assistance of the VTTMAA administration, which included the principal, a guidance counselor, the technology coordinator, and a school nurse, developed an application process for student participation in the Project SHARE program. To meet the recruitment criteria, students were required to have a grade point average in good standing, attend school regularly, obtain a teacher recommendation, and complete an essay describing their version of what a healthy community might look like. VTTMAA administration promoted the program widely and invited specific students to apply. The Team conducted recruitment interviews at the high school. As true academic partners in the Baltimore City schools, the Team underwent background checks, which are required for all teachers in Baltimore City.

Recruitment of motivated, committed students for the program was a factor crucial to its success. The Team relied heavily on its collaboration with VTTMAA staff to strategize how best to recruit and retain students. In its first year, 12 rising sophomores and juniors were selected to participate. VTTMAA staff had critical insight into the lives of the students and how the Team could address barriers to full participation in the project. To incentivize participation, the grant covered hourly wages for the students to participate in the yearlong program. T-shirts and notebook computers were provided for each student, and a room within the HS/HSL with tables, chairs, whiteboards, and lockers became the Project SHARE program's designated "space." Guidelines and expectations for class attendance, participation, and performance were established. Students received bus passes to use over the summer so they would not face a financial barrier in coming to the HS/HSL for classes after their school-issued student transit passes expired. All these decisions were collaborative and contributed to the students having the support they needed to be fully committed to the program.

Another key factor in recruiting and retaining student participants was engaging parents early on in the recruitment process. As part of the process, the Team visited the high school and gave a presentation to interested students and their families. This presentation, which was promoted to families through VTTMAA channels, portrayed the academic benefits of the program to students. Working together, staff at VTTMAA and the Team chose the students to participate in the program. Once students were accepted into the program, the Team again visited the school to deliver a presentation that reviewed the benefits of the program; gave an overview of the timeline, detailed program expectations, and student responsibilities; and discussed communication strategies. This presentation served to reengage parents as partners.

Parents also became involved in the Project SHARE Advisory Committee. As the program was being developed, the Team reached out to stakeholders and interested parties to assemble the Committee. In addition to parents, it consisted of representatives from VTTMAA (the school nurse and guidance counselor), a member of UMB's Outreach Council, Baltimore City Community College staff, and, eventually, the students themselves. This Committee, which met quarterly, was formed to keep communication lines open and to gather suggestions for program development.

Two cohorts of 12 students participated in the program annually. Each year, students received more than 150 hours of instruction supplemented by experiential learning activities. The students came to the HS/HSL after school and in the summer to attend classes developed just for them. Classes were delivered on social determinants of health, personal health records, family medical histories, evaluating health information, health literacy, presentation skills, health advocacy, health policy, health campaigns, outreach poster design, communication skills, and more. To complement the classroom-based learning, the program included field trips and other types of experiential learning.

CURRICULUM DESIGN

Curriculum development was led by the SHARE Project Manager/ Outreach Librarian with assistance from others. A diverse team of instructors included UMB faculty librarians from the HS/HSL's Services division, all of whom were experienced in the design and delivery of instruction and had years of experience collaborating with community partners to assess needs, design and deliver quality instruction, create support materials, and evaluate programs. Other participants included the HS/HSL executive director, staff from the Computing and Technology Division, and a community outreach coordinator from the NNLM SEA. The project also funded one intern per year at 10 hours/week. The interns, students in Towson University's Community Health and Health Administration program, contributed valuable administrative support and knowledge of community health theory and practice.

The Team leveraged expertise at UMB and from contacts throughout Baltimore to enrich the students' learning experiences. These invited speakers contributed expertise not found in the Library faculty. Guest lecturers, for instance, included community organizers and UMB School of Law students who led a class on how to think about advocacy and how to write effective advocacy letters. Students in the School of Pharmacy participated in a field trip to CVS to discuss how to shop for over-the-counter products. Members from community-based organizations made presentations to the students about the services they provided in the areas of homelessness, early childhood education, and more. The broad participation of instructors from within the HS/HSL, from UMB, and from the local community, enhanced the curriculum. Tapping into the expertise of the people most suited to deliver the message created energy around the project and enriched the curriculum with new voices and experiences.

Experiential Learning

Classroom learning was complemented by community-based experiential learning and social action projects. To design successful experiential learning opportunities throughout Baltimore, the Team needed to build upon existing community relationships and to develop new ones. From their work on previous outreach projects, the Team was able to build upon relationships with a variety of partners, including staff at homeless shelters, the Baltimore City Health Department, the University of Maryland Medical Center, and more. Student participation as exhibitors in a Baltimore Healthy Expo and field trips to community centers, a hospital, pharmacies, grocery stores, farmers' markets, an urban farm, and the NLM took careful planning with multiple partners to ensure that these active learning visits were successful.

Each cohort of students engaged in more than 10 outreach events per year. In the second year of the program, students initiated, led, and planned a successful health fair at VTTMAA with over 15 exhibitors and 300 student attendees. This social action project required the students to identify the exhibitors to participate in the fair, extend the invitation to attend, and manage the relationships. Planning this high-profile event was an important exercise in collaboration for the students. It also provided the students with an opportunity to establish new connections and work with new partners. These new partners included representatives from an urban farm (Real Food Farm), an organ donation group (Donate Life Maryland), The Y of Central Maryland, and a physician who offered weight/body mass index screenings. Through hands-on outreach events, students had a chance to apply their newly acquired advocacy skills toward promoting health at VTTMAA and in Baltimore neighborhoods.

At the completion of each of the yearlong programs, the HS/HSL hosted a formal capstone event honoring program accomplishments. Attendees included the many guest lecturers from within UMB, VTTMAA staff, partners from settings in Baltimore who worked with the Team to offer experiential learning, students' families, selected staff from the NLM, and Advisory Committee members. The capstone celebrated the success of the students and the collaborative work of the many partners who helped to make that success possible.

Online Curriculum

The Team was committed to creating a project that could be sustained and replicated. With this goal in mind, the Team designed an out-of-the-box-ready, modular curriculum that could be used anywhere in the nation. In the third year of the project, the Team applied what they had learned from working directly with VTTMAA students to create an online curriculum. The Team gathered best practices from 2 years in the classroom and out in the community, organized lesson content, and created a user-friendly website to showcase the modular curriculum. This freely available, web-based curriculum includes PowerPoint presentations, background readings, extracurricular learning activities, and social action projects. Each lesson's learning objectives aligned with *National Health Education Standard* objectives[8] and with selected objectives within *Healthy People 2020's* Adolescent Health topic.[9] The Team standardized the lesson plans into a template to present them in a uniform way. More than 12 faculty librarians participated in the curriculum development. Together, they developed 19 individual lessons, organized into six modules: Overview of Health Disparities, Quality Health Information, Taking Charge of Your Health, Smart Food Choices, Promoting Health and Wellness in Your Community, and Crafting and Delivering the Message. Lessons and modules were highly flexible and could be used stand-alone or in combination. The Project SHARE online curriculum debuted in September 2014.[10]

Collaboration played a two-part role in the development of the online curriculum. First, a diverse group of instructors covering a broad range of topics worked together to create a content-rich curriculum that spoke with one voice. Participating in regular team meetings, the instructors discussed curriculum components, design, and organization. The creation of a shared template ensured that instructors formatted their lesson plan components—learning objectives, class length, hands-on activities—in a uniform way. Second, the Team also recognized the importance of looking beyond the library staff including guest lecturers and other partners to contribute expertise and field knowledge. To convey the importance of collaboration to the curriculum, one of the important elements highlighted in each of the 19-class lesson plans was a suggestion from the instructor about key partners to include in the classroom.

NATIONAL AREA HEALTH EDUCATION CENTER ORGANIZATION HEALTH INFORMATION LITERACY PROJECT

In 2015, the National AHEC Organization (NAO) selected the SHARE curriculum for a 2-year national health information literacy project. The NAO provides multidisciplinary services to a range of people and partners—both students and practitioners—in medically underserved areas throughout the nation. The NAO's health information literacy project was implemented by six Area Health Education Centers (AHECs) in diverse settings across the United States—in urban, frontier, and tribal settings. The project addressed youth empowerment through building health information skills and social action projects. Nearly 100 students participated, the majority of whom came from the low-income and minority communities most affected by health disparities. Because the curriculum was modular, the project managers in each AHEC chose the lessons to adapt to their individual environments. During project implementation, the NLM's Specialized Information Services (SIS) collaborated with the NAO to evaluate the outreach program's effectiveness using an online pre- and posttest survey and postproject focus groups. Results of the evaluation showed that participating in the program improved students' understanding of health disparities, health information literacy, and interest in pursuing health careers, and communication and leadership skills.[11] The most successful projects had a high level of staff involvement and social action components.[11]

HS/HSL LISTENS

After the AHECs applied the SHARE curriculum in the field, the Team had the opportunity to hear directly from community health educators about the curriculum's successes and areas for development. After year one of the NAO's health information literacy project, the Team, prompted and supported by the NLM's SIS, worked with the AHECs to hear first-hand about their implementation experiences. The Team had ongoing and productive conversations with staff from the NAO describing the collective AHECs' implementation experiences. The Team followed this with one-on-one conversations with staff from individual AHECs focused on specific recommendations from the field. These conversations—rich with examples and detail—helped the Team envision what changes could be made to enrich the curriculum. While stretched thin, and often overcommitted, these community health educators made time to share their experiences to advance the progress of the project. The Team and the AHECs' community health educators shared a vision: improving the health literacy skills of underserved youth. This shared vision was a natural platform for collaboration.

After gathering feedback from the AHECs, the Team applied for and received funding from the Center for Public Service Communications (Agreement #2016-33) to expand and enrich the curriculum. Development of the curriculum and changes to the website were implemented by the HS/HSL project manager, an instructional designer, and a consultant in health literacy. The Team created a new health equity module, focusing on building healthy behaviors and student empowerment. This new module included lesson content incorporating solution-based discussions and encouraging student interactions. The Team improved lessons in health information literacy by incorporating activity-based discussions and creating exercises in which students applied real-life scenarios helping them experience the importance of comprehension skills to improved health. The SHARE curriculum's many activities, field trips, and social actions projects were reorganized, making them easier to locate on the website. To make the smart food choices module more challenging for high school students, the Team added additional content on the science of food labels. Changes to expand and enrich the curriculum took 5 months.

NEXT STEPS

In the next phase of the project, the Team will enhance the curriculum with added content based on recent research identifying significant or emerging public health concerns. The Team also aims to create and arrange experiential learning activities and social action projects by region and introduce new interactive learning activities incorporating mobile technology focusing on capturing students' stories. The vision is to create a platform through which students share content, enabling a peer-to-peer approach to promote health equity.

The Team will also focus on expanding the reach of the curriculum with an effective and strategic marketing campaign, highlighting the health advocacy curriculum's benefits: a field tested, out-of-the-box ready, modular format; step-by-step lesson plans with learning objectives tied to CDC's National Health Education Standards[8]; and examples of solution-based discussions, social action projects, and experiential learning activities.

The Team aims to collaborate with a variety of organizations at the national, regional, and local level to promote the online curriculum as a tool to be used in community-level interventions to improve health and wellness. The goal is to raise the profile of the curriculum by creating partnerships with organizations committed to promoting health equity. Furthermore, the Team aims to establish a community of practice, strengthening the relationships among groups applying the curriculum in the field. By developing an easy, interactive tool, individuals will be able to share stories, successes, challenges, and outcomes of using the curriculum in their settings. This online tool will provide a platform for support and inspiration as well as efficiencies in implementing the curriculum in diverse settings.

SUMMARY

Collaboration was key to the success of this project. The program vision was conceived in a collaborative work environment, funded by an NLM Information Resource Grant to Reduce Health Disparities, and developed with a community partner, VTTMAA. Classroom learning and experiential activities were implemented in a team setting with a variety of UMB and community partners. The modular online curriculum, designed for a wide audience, was used in NAO's nationally coordinated teen health information literacy project and evaluated with a partner—the NLM. Community health workers applying the curriculum in the field generously shared their expert advice and experiences with the Team. With funding from the Center for Public Service Communications, the Team then made enhancements to the curriculum. People and institutions with a shared vision—to improve the lives of underserved students—collaborated to promote health equity.

Advocacy and collaboration go hand in hand. Health equity will be achieved with collaborative, multiagency, and community efforts to ensure that all communities have fair access to the resources and opportunities necessary to be healthy.[12]

REFERENCES

1. Baltimore City Health Department. *Healthy Baltimore 2020: A Blueprint for Health.* Baltimore MD: Baltimore City Health Department; March 2017. Available from: https://health.baltimorecity.gov/sites/default/files/HB2020%20-%20April%202017.pdf.
2. Baltimore City Health Department. *2017 Neighborhood Health Profile for Southwest Baltimore.* Baltimore MD: Baltimore City Health Department; June 2017. Available from: https://health.baltimorecity.gov/sites/default/files/NHP%202017%20-%2051%20Southwest%20Baltimore%20(rev%206-9-17).pdf.

3. Baltimore City Health Department. *2017 Neighborhood Health Profile for North Baltimore/Guilford/Homeland*. Baltimore MD: Baltimore City Health Department; June 2017. Available from: https://health.baltimorecity.gov/sites/default/files/NHP%202017%20-%2039%20North%20Baltimore-Guilford-Homeland%20(rev%206-9-17).pdf.
4. University of Maryland Baltimore. *UMB Fast Facts*. Baltimore: University of Maryland Baltimore; 2017, 2016–2017. Available from: http://www.umaryland.edu/about-umb/umb-fast-facts/.
5. University of Maryland, Baltimore. *University of Maryland, Baltimore Strategic Plan 2017-2021*. Baltimore, MD: University of Maryland, Baltimore; 2017. Available from: https://www.umaryland.edu/media/umb/strategic-plan/pdfs/SP17-21-Strategic-Plan-Overview-v4-SINGLE-PAGES.pdf.
6. University of Maryland Health Science and Human Services Library. *HS/HSL Strategic Plan 2017-2021*. Baltimore: University of Maryland Baltimore; June 21, 2017, 2015–2017. Available from: http://www.hshsl.umaryland.edu/about/strategic.cfm.
7. Baltimore City Public Schools. *Vivien T. Thomas Medical Arts Academy School No. 429 School Profile - Spring 2017 Update*. Baltimore, MD: Baltimore City Public Schools; 2017 Spring. Available from: http://www.baltimorecityschools.org/cms/lib/MD01001351/Centricity/domain/8783/schoolprofiles/2017_18/20170517_Vivien_T_Thomas_School_Profile.pdf.
8. CDC: Centers for Disease Control and Prevention. *National Health Education Standards*. Atlanta: US Department of Health and Human Services; August 18, 2016, 2017. Available from: https://www.cdc.gov/healthyschools/sher/standards/index.htm.
9. HealthyPeople.gov: Healthy People 2020. *2020 Topics and Objectives: Adolescent Health*. Washington, DC: US Department of Health and Human Services, Office of Disease Prevention and Health Promotion; September 27, 2017, 2017, 2014. Available from: https://www.healthypeople.gov/2020/topics-objectives/topic/Adolescent-Health/objectives.
10. University of Maryland Health Science and Human Services Library. *Project SHARE Curriculum*. Baltimore: University of Maryland Baltimore; 2017. Available from: http://guides.hshsl.umaryland.edu/projectshare.
11. Keselman A, Chase R, Dutcher G, Kelly J, Scott J. Evaluation of Project SHARE, a youth health information literacy and leadership curriculum, implementation at six locations across the country. In: *2017 Medical Library Association Annual Meeting, Seattle, WA*. May 2017.
12. Baltimore City Health Department, Office of Epidemiology and Planning. *2010 Baltimore City Health Disparities Report Card*. Baltimore MD: Baltimore City Health Department; May 2010. Available from: http://baltimorehealth.org/wp-content/uploads/2016/06/2010_05_25_HDR-FINAL.pdf.

CHAPTER 8

Strengthening Strategic Planning Through Diverse Collaborations

M.J. Tooey[1], Aphrodite Bodycomb[1], Patricia G. Hinegardner[1], Alexa Mayo[1], J. Dale Prince[2]

[1]Health Sciences and Human Services Library, University of Maryland, Baltimore, Baltimore, MD, United States; [2]Louisiana State University Health Sciences Center, Division of Libraries, New Orleans, LA, United States

BACKGROUND

The University of Maryland, Baltimore (UMB), experienced an evolution in the creation of its strategic plan over the years. With the arrival of a new UMB administration in 2011, a renewed effort was made to develop a strategic plan meaningful to the entire UMB community. With six professional and graduate-level schools and a strong history of school autonomy, this was a challenging endeavor; however, a plan was developed focusing on key initiatives of UMB.

The Health Sciences and Human Services Library (HS/HSL) at the UMB has a long and strong history of regular strategic planning going back more than 2 decades. In 2011 when UMB leadership changed, the HS/HSL was poised to embark on a new strategic planning process. A Team, consisting of the executive director and the associate directors for Services, Resources, Technology, Administration, and the Regional Medical Library, had already begun thinking about its next major strategic planning effort and was exploring new, innovative, and collaborative ways to develop the new plan.

Since the new UMB administration had embarked almost immediately on a strategic planning process, the Team was afforded an opportunity to refine, reflect, and redesign the process. Before planning, the Team felt it was critical to await the completion of the new UMB strategic plan. The UMB plan would then serve as a guide for critical elements of the HS/HSL plan, as strong, successful library strategic planning should align with institutional strategic plans and imperatives.

Strategic Collaborations in Health Sciences Libraries
ISBN 978-0-08-102258-0
https://doi.org/10.1016/B978-0-08-102258-0.00008-2
Copyright © 2019 Jean P. Shipman and M.J. Tooey. Published by Elsevier Limited. All rights reserved.

ISSUES AND DRIVERS FOR HS/HSL STRATEGIC PLANNING

The strategic planning approach frequently taken by libraries is to internally develop a plan and share it with their user community. This was confirmed by an internal discussion on the Association of Academic Health Sciences Libraries discussion list in 2010. This "library knows best" strategic planning approach distances the library from user needs and collaborative conversations regarding what is important and valuable to users.

Two major environmental factors influenced the decision to approach strategic planning in a new outwardly focused, inclusive, and collaborative fashion:

1. A new leadership and political climate at UMB focused on collaboration and inclusivity. In addition to the focus within the new UMB strategic plan, there was also renewed statewide interest in a closer relationship between UMB and the University of Maryland, College Park.
2. The second environmental factor was the swiftly evolving library landscape which included the rapid growth and evolution of digital environments; eroding financial situations in libraries, universities, and in research funding; increased focus on user engagement; shifting priorities; and the increased use of collaborative and interdepartmental teams to identify and meet library user needs.

THE MEANING OF COLLABORATION FOR THE HS/HSL STRATEGIC PLANNING

In "the library knows best" model, development of a strategic plan occurs within the library with final approval by a university administrative body or library committee, with very little collaboration. As the HS/HSL strategic planning process evolved, regular Team meetings revealed many different opportunities for collaborations.

By examining and questioning the strategic planning process and carefully considering the environmental factors, a more inclusive and collaborative process was developed. This process encouraged collaborations with a diverse group of people throughout. A liberal interpretation of Merriam-Webster's definition of "collaborate" was embraced. The definition says collaborate means "to work jointly with others or together especially in an intellectual endeavor."[1] The Team interpreted collaboration boldly, by collaborating with those external to the HS/HSL; with those internal to the HS/HSL; and with relevant individuals and groups across and beyond UMB. This interpretation supported conversations with a wide-ranging group of faculty, staff, students, individuals, and communities of interest. It became a very flexible and fluid process, changing and adapting with every conversation.

THE PROCESS

Overview

The Team assumed responsibility for strategic planning. The initial collaboration for the first round of the new HS/HSL strategic plan was between the UMB vice president for administration, who had been in charge of developing the UMB strategic plan, and the HS/HSL executive director. They met to review the process, approach, and format for developing a plan. With assurances that the planning process was in sync with the UMB plan, the Team was ready to begin.

The Team deliberated over the best approach to elicit information from constituents with the focus on how the HS/HSL could contribute to their success. This user-focused approach meant that the Team needed to listen carefully to understand constituent needs. A "strategic listening" tour of the UMB community was envisioned in which the Team visited key constituents to learn about their future goals and challenges and the ways they gauged success. The Team understood the HS/HSL is most successful when partners and constituents are successful. Question development was a key component of the process. Several members of the Team had formal training in and experience facilitating focus groups, including developing effective, open-ended questions to elicit big-picture insights. It was important that the listening tour questions address strategic direction rather than current operational issues. The Team devoted many hours to refining the questions, ensuring that the responses focused on a broad vision for user success.

Ideas for expanding the collaborative process were also considered. Although important to get the UMB community and constituent input, it was equally important to engage the HS/HSL staff in the process. The Team synthesized input from the strategic listening tour, creating a draft of the strategic plan. Seven department heads—the next leadership level in the HS/HSL—then assisted in identifying specific operational goals. In the final stages of the strategic planning process, all staff reviewed and discussed the draft plan to provide feedback, identify issues, and ensure buy-in.

Details of External Collaboration

The Team embarked on a strategic listening tour involving the senior leadership at UMB, including the president, deans, and key administrators from research, communications, accountability, finance, technology, and economic development. Thirteen individuals were in the initial strategic listening group. The sessions were designed to provide UMB leaders with ample opportunity to speak to the strategic listening team. Open-ended questions were developed and emphasized. Strategic listening teams consisted of the HS/HSL executive director, who served as facilitator, and another member of the Team, who was responsible for listening carefully, asking clarifying questions, and taking notes. Three questions were posed to the UMB senior leadership (see Appendix A.1). At the end of each session, participants were asked to identify other key stakeholders who should attend future listening sessions.

Using information provided from these sessions, the Team brainstormed about other stakeholders who needed to be involved from all levels of UMB. The identification of key groups, such as student, faculty, and staff organizations, and technology groups, provided a broad perspective on the complexity of the work ahead. Discussions and decisions were made about the best strategy for meeting with the identified individuals and groups. A multi-method approach was determined to be the best way of gathering information. Individual meetings, group meetings, town halls, and online surveys were all used to gather information.

Over 25 people participated in the next phase of the listening tour. Hour-long focus group–style meetings were organized to obtain information from this diverse group, including faculty and staff from each of the schools and from the Office of Research Development, Campus IT, Community Outreach Services, and more. Three meetings were planned at various times to accommodate participant schedules. Two questions started the discussion (see Appendix A.2). People were asked to think in terms of expertise, resources, and place. The HS/HSL executive director facilitated the discussion and members of the Team took detailed notes. These discussions were wide-ranging and provided useful information for the HS/HSL strategic plan.

Students also needed to be heard. Working through the Student Government Association, Graduate Student Association, and through the HS/HSL's usual promotion mechanisms, students were invited to attend an open forum. It was hosted in the HS/HSL in late afternoon and about 15 students from the School of Nursing, School of Medicine, and the Graduate School attended. In the past, students had been interested in extending HS/HSL hours, which required campus safety input. Campus Police were invited to participate in the discussion. During the session, three questions were posed to the students (see Appendix A.3). The hour-long open forum was conversational and very informative.

One of the final stops in the listening tour was a Faculty/Staff Town Hall. Faculty and staff from around UMB were invited to attend a brown bag, hour-long discussion. This method was not so successful in gathering information as were the targeted individual and focus group—style meetings. Some valuable feedback was obtained as several faculty wrote directly to the HS/HSL executive director with their thoughts on the future directions for the HS/HSL. In the promotion of the town hall, three questions were included (see Appendix A.4).

Before concluding the year-long listening tour, the Team developed and implemented a survey providing one last opportunity for any member of the UMB community to participate in the process and help shape the HS/HSL's future. It included four open-ended questions (see Appendix A.5). There were 85 responses to the online survey posted on the HS/HSL's web page. This marked the end of the external information gathering phase of the project.

Themes

The data collected from the UMB community were reviewed for commonalities, and broad themes were identified. Some suggestions and themes were operational enhancements that could be addressed and implemented immediately. For example, weekend and morning hours were changed to accommodate requests for the HS/HSL to be open more hours.

Other themes were used to inform the drafting of the strategic plan. These included the importance of the expertise offered at the HS/HSL; the need for more online resources; identifying and developing partnerships with other offices at UMB such as the Office of Research and Development and the Center for Information Technology; and promoting HS/HSL services to staff in addition to students and faculty. The "library as place" was a key theme. Having a variety of spaces with comfortable seating conducive to individual study and collaborative learning was mentioned often. People saw the HS/HSL as a safe place, a place for collaboration, and as a cultural space engaging the community with events and programs. The overall feedback received through the listening tour was that the HS/HSL was a valued resource and partner supportive of UMB, school, and individual priorities. HS/HSL space was also highly regarded. One major recommendation was for the HS/HSL to improve promotion of activities, services, and resources.

Details of Internal Collaboration

Once input from the UMB community was collected and reviewed, the HS/HSL executive director organized a retreat for the Team to (1) determine how to engage library department heads and all 57 staff in the strategic planning process; (2) develop the content and format of the plan; (3) promote the plan to the UMB community; and (4) develop a timeline for completion. The 2011–16 UMB strategic plan,[2] samples of strategic plans from other university libraries, and summary documents from the listening tour were reviewed.

The Team determined four main themes reflective of the UMB plan: (1) research, (2) teaching and learning, (3) community, and (4) culture. Because department heads were involved in the day-to-day operations and management of the HS/HSL, they were asked to identify and write goals under each theme. Their experience and expertise was a perfect match for this task. Once reviewed and finalized by the Team, the goals were incorporated into the plan.

The Team aimed to develop a vibrant mission and vision statement. "Expertise," "Resources," and "Place" concisely captured the essence of the HS/HSL and were used to drive the mission statement. The Team created a simple statement:

> *The Health Sciences and Human Services Library meets the information needs of our diverse communities through provision of expertise, resources, services and an environment supportive of the University's values and mission.*[3]

A different approach was used to develop the vision statement. Each of the five associate directors crafted a vision statement for the HS/HSL as part of the process. The department heads then reviewed all the statements, creating a single statement incorporating language from several of the suggested visions. This collaborative approach resulted in a stronger statement:

> *We will create a dynamic, collaborative, and innovative knowledge environment focused on excellence in expertise, service, and resource access and creation, relevant to and advancing university priorities. We will advance the library as a vibrant intellectual and cultural hub for the university.*[3]

With the mission and vision statements complete, the Team turned to writing the values statement for the plan. After reviewing the value statements from the UMB's strategic plan and an earlier HS/HSL strategic plan, the Team wrote a concise values statement:

Strive for excellence.

Collaborate to enhance knowledge.

Anticipate, respond, and evolve to meet the needs of our users.

Promote a diverse environment marked by integrity, inclusiveness and respect.

Lead in the creation and dissemination of knowledge in our professional communities.[3]

The next step was outlining strategies to successfully achieve the goals of the plan. The University of North Carolina Libraries' strategic plan included a section that resonated with many of the strategies identified as essential for achieving the HS/HSL vision.[4] These North Carolina strategies were refined to become the HS/HSL's "Strategies for Achieving Success" (see Table 8.1).

Table 8.1 University of Maryland, Baltimore library's "strategies for achieving success"

Prepare staff for new roles through programming and training opportunities.
Promote a collaborative/collegial work environment.
Recruit and retain a diverse, knowledgeable, and flexible workforce.
Encourage and sustain expertise, skills, curiosity, and commitment.
Adopt a lifecycle planning approach that ensures optimal and user-oriented technology resources.
Evaluate, acquire, and support the technologies that users need to discover, create, use, and preserve information.
Create an overall plan that aligns with the Library's strategic themes.
Reimagine and redesign Library environments through a continuous, evidence-based process.
Conduct regular needs assessments for service improvements and planning, incorporating users into the decision-making process.
Use data to demonstrate the value of services, collections, and environments.
Through an effective communication and promotion program, build awareness of and support for the Library.
Advocate for the Library as an essential component of the university's infrastructure.
Strive for a stable and appropriate funding environment.
Diversify funding sources through pursuit of grant, contract, and other opportunities.

The completed draft of the HS/HSL's 2015/2020 Strategic Plan consisted of a mission and vision statement, four broad themes with accompanying goals, and strategies for achieving success.

Involving all 57 HS/HSL staff members in the strategic planning process was important for promoting interdepartmental collaboration, fostering buy-in, and for gaining a better understanding of how staff members view their roles. Eventually, the plan would be used to inform personal development plans so this engagement was imperative. A 2-hour all-staff event was organized to review and comment on the themes and goals developed by the Team and department heads. The meeting was held in a large meeting room, set up with five conference room tables. As each person arrived, they were given a number corresponding to a specific table. By randomly assigning each person a number, people from different departments were seated together at each table. This provided an opportunity for broader discussions. The staff were asked to consider eight questions (See Appendix A.6). Each group chose a recorder and reporter. Although the groups discussed all the themes, each table was assigned a primary theme to champion and report on. Based on these discussions and questions, minor improvements and clarifications were made to the strategic plan, especially in clarifying specific language.

Several weeks later, a second meeting was held. Staff members were randomly assigned to tables and asked to discuss the "Strategies For Achieving Success." The Team provided the list of strategies focusing on staff expertise, technologies, physical spaces and virtual environments, communicating library value, and funding. Staff members were asked to think of ways to help implement the strategies, focusing on the UMB and HS/HSL big picture, not specific to their division. Each table was assigned one strategy to champion. Both staff sessions saw positive participation by all members, were productive, and added to the refinement of the plan through clarification of strategies.

To assess the effectiveness of the staff meetings in support of the process, a survey was sent to all HS/HSL staff. The results of this 10 question survey (Appendix A.7) revealed that after the meeting discussion, staff were (1) confident or very confident the plan set a visionary, viable, and achievable direction and (2) were confident or very confident their division could develop its own strategic plan supportive of the HS/HSL plan. Staff felt their individual performance goals, which are reviewed and updated annually, could easily be aligned with the HS/HSL plan. Staff gave high marks to the effectiveness of the meeting and to the draft of the plan.

Once the themes and goals were finalized, the plan was reviewed by each division, and specific, measurable objectives were tied to each goal. Each division then prepared a presentation that highlighted key objectives for their area. HS/HSL staff meetings were held to showcase objectives from each division, from a "family feud"–style session highlighting the Services Division's objectives, to the individual creativity of several members of the Computing and Technology Services Division who used props including frogs, wigs, and more—creativity reigned! The presentations were a great morale booster and, based on the responses to the staff survey, solidified staff buy-in.

After multiple collaborations, hours of strategic listening, reviewing notes and survey results, refining, discussing and writing, the *Health Sciences & Human Services Library, University of Maryland Strategic Plan* was published in September 2015.

THE ONLY CONSTANT IS CHANGE

No sooner was the HS/HSL strategic plan completed, when UMB announced, early in 2016, it was time to completely revise its plan to reflect new priorities and directions. Each school and unit was required to create plans aligned with UMB's. As a consequence, the recently completed and published 2015/2020 HS/HSL plan dropped into limbo. While UMB developed its new plan, the Team found itself engaged, once again, with the strategic planning process only a few months after completing its own.

Upon completion of UMB's new strategic planning process and the publication of the revised UMB plan,[5] the Team and the department heads met for a day-long retreat in November 2016 to review the existing 2015/2020 HS/HSL plan, rooted in the four original strategic planning themes of research, teaching and learning, community, and culture. The group reviewed the 2015/2020 HS/HSL plan to align it with UMB's six new themes of health, justice, and social impact; research and scholarship; student success; inclusive excellence; partnership and collaboration; and efficiency, effectiveness, and assessment. During the retreat, the Team and the department heads restructured the HS/HSL's 2015/2020 plan, rearranging the goals and strategies into the six new broad themes. As required by UMB, an internal document was created casting each goal as SMART (Specific, Measurable, Attainable, Results-based, and Time-bound).[6]

In the long term, the work already done on the 2015/2020 plan was fortuitous. It meant the HS/HSL had a running start and did not have to build its 2017–21 UMB-aligned plan from the ground up. Additionally, the Team and department heads already had experience writing SMART goals. The head-start created by these circumstances resulted in other positive effects as well.

The research and assessment librarian was tasked with entering the revised HS/HSL SMART goals into Compliance Assist, the system used by UMB to gauge adherence to and completion of strategic plans. The UMB director of planning collaborated to review the new plan to ensure alignment. Early completion, collaboration, and being an early adopter of the compliance system ultimately led to the HS/HSL's plan being held up as a model for the entire UMB community.

DISCUSSION

A practical aspect of assigning SMART goals to the plan was accountability. Have goals been met? Have they been superseded or revised? As goals are completed, they are replaced with current aspirations. The result is constant revision and growth of the plan. The HS/HSL does not propose to rest on a static set of strategies, but will collaborate constantly with stakeholders to review and ensure relevance with plans, regularly repeating the strategic listening initiative. It is only by collaborating with stakeholders that the Library can validate current direction and learn of new ways to ensure the success of its users.

The HS/HSL's 2017–21 strategic plan, like UMB's, is a pyramidal structure, with the themes and strategic goals visible to the public.[7] This portion, which is displayed on websites and in trifolds, is the overview—the elevator speech version. The bulk of the plan lies at the HS/HSL divisional level. The divisional strategic plans operationalize the themes and indicate the specific activities each will conduct in support of the themes. The operational plans are more extensive, granular, and tied to individual goals. Extending accountability to the staff level has had the effect of making the success of the plan a collaborative effort, with each staff member playing a part. The HS/HSL is intentional about aligning individual development plans to the goals of its strategic plan.

The collaborative planning initiative and new strategic plan have already had an impact on the Library. This includes the areas of professional development, responsiveness to user needs, improved communication, and user input.

The integration of the operational part of the HS/HSL's strategic plan includes maintaining a highly knowledgeable base of employees to support UMB. A SMART goal in the HS/HSL strategic plan requires each HS/HSL employee to participate in at least one professional development opportunity per year. Supervisors are required to develop plans for their employees and track their progress.

An example of the plan's responsiveness to the needs of UMB resulted from being strategically aware of future needs. After consulting with the President's Entrepreneurship and Innovation Fellows, who spent a year researching the best ways for UMB to prepare students for entrepreneurial careers, the HS/HSL created a task force to develop the UMB Entrepreneur Toolkit.[8] Using the "strategic listening" model, the task force sought the input of key individuals across UMB, creating a guide to provide potential entrepreneurs and innovators with useful information and helpful links. The Fellows named the HS/HSL one of the most entrepreneurial enterprises on campus.

During the strategic planning process, a constant theme heard by the Team was that the Library needed to improve communications. The Library formed the Effective Communications Committee that meets monthly to discuss news from the HS/HSL and where the news is most appropriately placed. Additionally, this Committee evaluates web usage and HS/HSL branding. The Committee realized surveys and inquiries need not be huge or time consuming to gather relevant and pertinent information for a successful strategic planning process.

Through the strategic planning process, it was learned that users were interested in providing input and guidance to the HS/HSL. As a result, instead of one large HS/HSL advisory committee, topically focused advisory task forces have been formed to assist with collection development and with the growth of an innovation space. These focused task forces are perfect examples of engaging experts in the user community in collaborative projects.

FUTURE IMPROVEMENT

A leitmotif to the library strategic planning process is "How to do better?" How does the HS/HSL serve, engage, and collaborate with stakeholders in innovative and meaningful ways? How does the HS/HSL engage staff members and encourage them to be the best they can be? The Team identified four areas for scrutiny in this regard: speed and agility, ongoing assessment, constant validation with HS/HSL faculty and staff, and ongoing productive collaboration with stakeholders to identify where they are reflected in the plan.

Agility can be an issue in crafting strategic plans. How best to prevent another extended process? The primary strategy is to look at a strategic plan as a living document. The decision to create a plan and collect data takes time. Stakeholders are not immediately available and collecting data from them may take months. Continuous engagement with stakeholders ensures growth and validation of the current plan. The HS/HSL employs many just-in-time data-collection methods: online surveys, such as the Library Genie where HS/HSL users list three wishes regarding library service, and informal surveys where a simple question is asked on a whiteboard and passersby respond with tally marks or comments. Through the use of focused querying, all first-year students are surveyed regarding thoughts about the HS/HSL annually. These surveys contribute a substantial amount to the knowledge the HS/HSL has about its users. Some of it is very humbling. The Team remains alert to new UMB leaders, and movers and shakers, mining them for new ideas soon upon arrival and building relationships.

Ongoing assessments are a good practice and happen at the UMB level through Compliance Assist Review and at the HS/HSL level through divisional, departmental, and individual review. The Team meets biannually to go over the goals to determine completion, relevance, or change in direction. New goals are added based upon divisional trajectories. The cycle begins anew with the engagement of all members of the Team who validate new directions.

The success of the plan is validated by the satisfaction of stakeholders. Continued collaboration with them is a way to measure satisfaction and gather continuous feedback. Through collaborative engagement with the community for problem solving, project partnerships, and advancing user success, the stakeholders have become intimate parts of HS/HSL processes, sharing ideas and serving as ambassadors to their communities.

Members of the HS/HSL faculty and staff are essential collaborative stakeholders, perhaps the most important ones. Through engagement in the planning processes, open information sharing, and growing expertise, HS/HSL faculty and staff have become trusted empowered advocates. In early

2018, the HS/HSL administered the Association of Research Library's ClimateQUAL[9] survey to gauge the perceptions of HS/HSL staff regarding inclusion and organizational culture.

CONCLUSION

The collaborative strategic planning process was a multifaceted approach to developing a meaningful strategic plan. The process engaged the community and the HS/HSL faculty and staff, It was concerned about ensuring the success of everyone involved, and provided the HS/HSL with a roadmap for new and continued conversations about what makes it vital and dynamic.

The collaborative strategic planning process discussed in this chapter can be modified and used in different types of settings. Key elements of the process include broad collaboration, a focus on the success of stakeholders, commitment to listening, and expertise in data collection methodologies.

What was learned? Use a variety of methods to gather data. Be agile and quick. Do not be afraid to engage users in any way that answers the question—no one way is always right—change things up. Assess and validate results. Do not be afraid of failure. The end result is always better with multiple views and is enriched by collaboration.

APPENDIX: QUESTIONS

A.1 Individual Meetings—University Leadership (Deans, Senior Administrators)

1. What library expertise, resources, or building components are critical to your unit's success?
2. Consider your strategic plan and future directions. As a partner in your success, what expertise, resources or building elements could or should we provide?
3. What else would you like to tell us or share with us?

A.2 Group Meetings—Selected Individuals—Diverse Group That Included Faculty and Staff From Each of the Schools and From the Office of Research Development, Campus IT, Community Outreach Services and More

1. What should the HS/HSL continue to do?
2. What should the HS/HSL do in the future?

A.3 Open Forum—Students

1. Please tell us what your ideas are about library hours including late night, 24-hour access, and badge-swipe access to the building.
2. What are your safety concerns as they relate to the library?
3. What else would you like to see in the way of services and learning spaces?

A.4 Town Hall—Faculty/Staff

1. What are we doing well?
2. What can we improve or do more?
3. What does the library of the future look like to you? What expertise should we have? What resources should we provide? What about new technologies? And what about the building?

A.5 Survey—Campus

1. What is the HS/HSL doing well? How do we add value to your work? What should we continue doing?
2. Where could the HS/HSL improve or do more? Are there enhancements to our expertise, resources, or space we should consider?
3. What does the "library" of the future look like to you? Please think of the library in the broadest possible sense—expertise, services, resources, technology, and space.
4. Is there anything else you would like to share with us to help guide us toward the future?

A.6 HS/HSL Staff Meeting—Faculty Librarians and Staff

1. Do you feel this theme and its goals are clear?
2. What about this theme and its goals excites you?
3. What about this theme and its goals makes you apprehensive?
4. Is there anything you would change about this goal? Add? Subtract?
5. How would you explain this theme and its goals to our constituents?
6. How do you see this theme/goals applying across the HS/HSL?
7. How would you apply this theme/goals within your division?
8. Personal reflection: How would you develop your own personal and professional goals aligned with this theme?

A.7 Survey—Faculty Librarians and Staff

1. Are you
   Choices: library staff, library faculty
2. The division I work in is
   Choices: CATS, Library Administration, Resources, Services, SE/A RML
3. After reviewing and discussing the draft strategic plan, I am confident it sets a visionary, viable, and achievable direction for the HS/HSL.
   Choices: very confident, confident, not confident
4. After reviewing and discussing the draft strategic plan, I am confident my division can develop its own strategic plan supportive of the HS/HSL plan.
   Choices: very confident, confident, not confident
5. After reviewing and discussing the draft strategic plan, I am confident I can develop personal and professional goals that fit within my divisional plan and within the HS/HSL's plan.
   Choices: very confident, confident, not confident
6. The time spent in the strategic plan review meeting was time well spent.
   Choices: agree, disagree
7. The amount of time spent (2 hours) was:
   Choices: too long, too short, just right.
8. The format of the 2 hours (random group assignment, introduction, background, small group discussion, reporting out/discussion) supported the work that needed to be done.
   Choices: agree, disagree
9. I would be interested in viewing the plan every year.
   Choices: Yes, No
10. After thinking about the July 28th strategic plan review session, here are some additional thoughts.

REFERENCES

1. Merriam-Webster. *Collaborate*. MA: Merriam-Webster Springfield; 2018. Available from: https://www.merriam-webster.com/dictionary/collaborate.
2. University of Maryland, Baltimore. *University of Maryland, Baltimore Strategic Plan 2011-2016*. Baltimore: University of Maryland; 2017. Available from: http://hdl.handle.net/10713/3904.

3. University of Maryland, Baltimore. *Health Sciences & Human Services Library, University of Maryland, Baltimore. Strategic Plan (2015/2020)*. Baltimore: University of Maryland; 2017. Available from: http://hdl.handle.net/10713/7169.
4. UNC University Libraries. *The Library and the Mission of the University 2013-2018*. Chapel Hill: University of North Carolina at Chapel Hill; 2013. Available from: http://library.unc.edu/wp-content/uploads/2013/07/13-3156-LIB-Libraries-5-Year-Plan_d13.pdf.
5. University of Maryland, Baltimore. *University of Maryland, Baltimore Strategic Plan 2017-2021*. Baltimore: University of Maryland; 2017. Available from: http://hdl.handle.net/10713/7170.
6. Conzemius A, O'Neil J. *The Power of SMART Goals: Using Goals to Improve Student Learning*. Bloomington (IN): Solution Tree Press; 2006, 232 p.
7. University of Maryland, Baltimore. *Health Sciences and Human Services Library Strategic Plan 2017-2021: Expertise, Resources, Place*. Baltimore: University of Maryland; 2017. Available from: http://hdl.handle.net/10713/7378.
8. University of Maryland, Baltimore. *UMB Entrepreneur Toolkit*. Baltimore (MD): University of Maryland; January 11, 2018. Available from: http://guides.hshsl.umaryland.edu/entretoolkit.
9. ClimateQUAL. *Organizational Climate and Diversity Assessment*. Washington (DC): Association of Research Libraries; 2017. Available from: https://www.climatequal.org/home.

CHAPTER 9

e-channel: A Platform for Disseminating the Scholarly Output of Innovators

Jean P. Shipman[1], **Christy Jarvis**[2]
[1]Global Library Relations, GSN, Elsevier, Cottonwood Heights, UT, United States; [2]Information Resources & Digital Initiatives, Spencer S. Eccles Health Sciences Library, University of Utah, Salt Lake City, UT, United States

BACKGROUND

The Spencer S. Eccles Health Sciences Library (EHSL) is responsible for advancing the educational, health care, and research efforts of University of Utah (UU) Health. Located in the heart of the health campus, its faculty and staff partner with the schools of medicine and dentistry, the colleges of nursing, pharmacy, and health, and the University's hospitals and clinics. Before 2012, the EHSL building housed a sizable print collection. In 2013, witnessing the dwindling use of its print resources, EHSL made the tactical decision to eliminate the vast majority of its print books and journals.[2] EHSL decided to relinquish its traditional role of collecting books in favor of collecting and connecting people through sharing library and office space and building a collaboration space. Staff members, freed from ongoing maintenance of the stacks, were able to redirect their efforts to seeking partners with whom the EHSL could collaborate on future projects driving innovation and discovery at the institution. The reclaimed physical space allowed the EHSL to invite those strategic partners into the building and focus on becoming the central hub for interprofessional and innovative collaborations.

Working in close proximity with University innovators facilitated EHSL's involvement in key institutional initiatives and projects. As EHSL became increasingly involved with campus innovation efforts, EHSL faculty soon became aware of the unique information needs and professional challenges of these individuals. Chief among them is the lack of publishing opportunities for disseminating their work. Traditional journal publishing focuses on research outcomes and is typically not receptive to publishing manuscripts or objects devoted to medical innovation output such as process improvements,

Strategic Collaborations in Health Sciences Libraries
ISBN 978-0-08-102258-0
https://doi.org/10.1016/B978-0-08-102258-0.00009-4
Copyright © 2019 Jean P. Shipman and M.J. Tooey. Published by Elsevier Limited. All rights reserved.

new technologies, brainstormed ideas, digital therapeutics (e.g., health applications and games), and other similar projects—both successes and failures. A literature search failed to produce a journal dedicated to medical innovations. This coupled with conversations with innovators at conferences confirmed a scholarly venue was needed. Building on the recommendations of a commissioned report by consulting firm, Delta Think, Inc., examining nontraditional publishing opportunities, EHSL faculty and staff met to discuss ways of addressing the lack of dissemination options for innovative work. The decision was made to create a nontraditional platform, e-channel, to collect and publicize the work of innovators across many disciplines, but particularly the health sciences. A partnership between gamers, EHSL faculty, and staff resulted in the creation of a multimedia platform soliciting and disseminating the work of innovators from various organizations and disciplines.

PLATFORM COLLABORATION

One of the first partners to share space in the EHSL building was The Therapeutic Games and Apps Lab (The GApp Lab).[3] The GApp Lab comprises Entertainment Arts & Engineering (EAE) graduate students and is a collaboration between EAE, the Center for Medical Innovation (CMI), and EHSL. While The GApp Lab focus primarily on the research, development, and production of interactive, medically focused games and apps, the expertise and skills of its members made them logical collaborators for the development of the e-channel platform. EHSL negotiated a contract with The GApp Lab including 1400 hours of e-channel site design work from a student team consisting of an engineer, an artist/designer, a producer, and a research assistant working under the direction of a faculty mentor. The completed project, illustrated in Fig. 9.1, was delivered to EHSL in early 2015.

The homegrown platform designed by The GApp Lab was the launch point for e-channel's development and served as the inspiration for collaborative projects going forward. In 2016, the platform for e-channel ultimately migrated to a more flexible and easily modified one—WordPress (see Fig. 9.2) to accommodate the rapid growth of content. Moving from a homegrown interface built using JavaScript Object Notation to a commercially available one offered many more attractive features such as usage statistics, access tiering rights, and a robust search engine capable of searching across different content formats to enhance discovery. It also eased adding new content as an entire new interface component does not have to be built each time. It is notable that

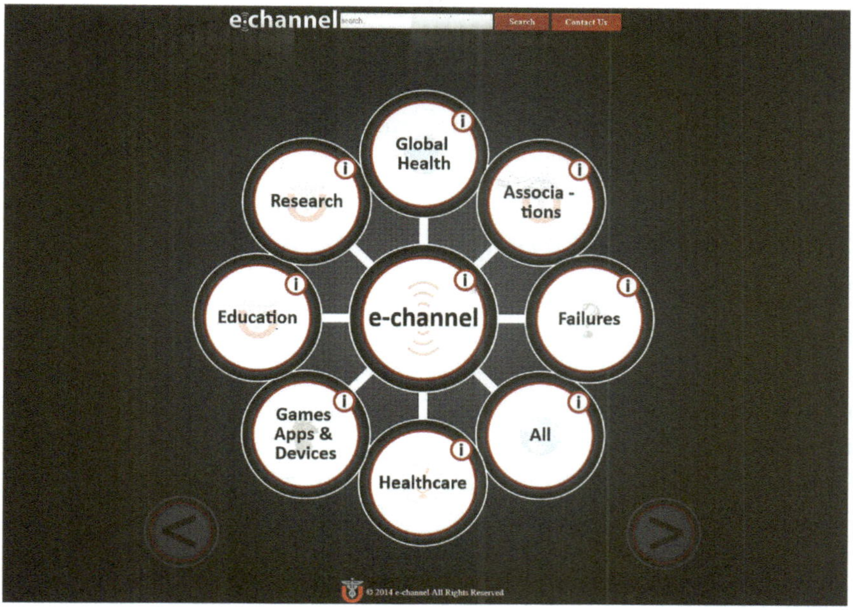

Figure 9.1 e-channel Home Page, Version 1, 2015 © e-channel.

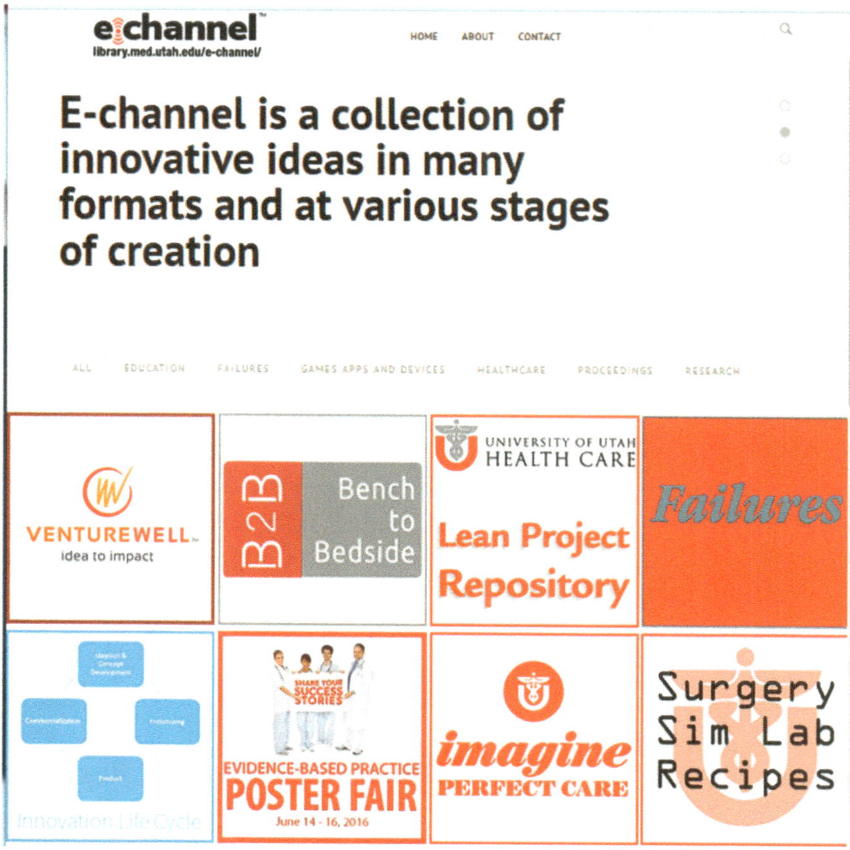

Figure 9.2 e-channel Home Page, Version 2, 2016 © e-channel.

e-channel—a platform dedicated to collaborative and innovative work—was itself the product of a fruitful partnership between the EHSL and other institutional departments.

CONTENT COLLABORATIONS—LOCAL PARTNERSHIPS

Center for Medical Innovation

As this was the original unit housed within the remodeled EHSL print collection space, it was natural the first entry for e-channel was the output created by this innovation center. CMI consists of three subunits—the annual Bench to Bedside (B2B) student medical device competition, a Skills Center or simulation center used primarily by surgeons to practice various skills and operating techniques, and The GApp Lab.

Bench to Bedside

Each year a student-driven medical device competition occurs in the spring with a capstone event held at the Utah state capitol building. Teams are given $500 and around 6 months to create a prototype device, conduct market research and generate a business plan, and obtain a provisional patent. Judges are gathered from throughout the University to view team video pitches prior to the capstone and then to personally interview teams at the event. Cash prizes totaling over $70,000 are awarded, including one from the Library Innovation Team (LIT) comprising representatives from all three University libraries—enabling teams to reinvest earnings to further develop their products. Top winners are granted University commercialization support to enter the market. The EHSL has videotaped the pre-capstone pitches and has encouraged the B2B student leaders to inform teams of the services and resources offered by the LIT. Library faculty present at B2B workshops and consult on identifying "prior art"—proof that an idea or invention is already known. Librarians also help identify evidence to support product need and development, and market research to aid in business plan creations. Resulting B2B pitch videos, annual reports, and photos are captured and preserved in e-channel to provide a one-stop-source for outputs from this now international competition.

Skills Center

The Skills Center houses a lot of simulators and training devices. Educational sessions are frequently conducted by University and outside instructors for surgeons, anesthesiologists, and other health-care professionals. The Skills

Center's one claim to fame is to create low-cost training tools to supplement the more expensive simulators. Their collections of "Surgery Sim Lab Recipes" are hosted on e-channel. Future e-channel content will include more of the Center's instructional materials supporting low-end simulations.

The GApp Lab

The aforementioned The GApp Lab, which partnered with EHSL to bring the vision of e-channel to life, remains an ongoing collaborator. Student teams submit "wrap kits" to e-channel for preservation and dissemination.[4] These multi-format "wrap kits" consist of various game design elements, such as artwork, style guides, and demo videos so the research and processes part of game development are documented for the future. Before The GApp Lab's collaboration with EHSL via e-channel, most of these important data sets were lost as graduating students would leave the institution, grant funds would run out, or programming attempts would fail. This loss of historical documentation of obstacles encountered, problems solved, and decisions made regarding game development meant future The GApp Lab teams were unable to build on the work of their predecessors. By partnering with EHSL to collection, organize, preserve, and share their "wrap kits," The GApp Lab is able to ensure mistakes, and triumphs of previous teams are passed on to future generations of innovators at the institution. This dissemination of knowledge via e-channel has a positive impact on The GApp Lab's ability to fulfill its mission of developing games and apps to improve patient care.

Lean Project Repository

Many institutions are looking toward applying Lean principles to eliminate waste within their institutions and to gain more cost efficiency. In 2013, Dr. Vivian Lee, then Senior Vice President of the Health System, CEO of the UU Hospital and Dean of the School of Medicine, commissioned the UU School of Business to train four cohorts of health leaders in Lean principles. The resulting project summaries—or A3 templates—were collected and disseminated via e-channel. Resulting professional journal publications, if written, have been linked to the project summaries.

Games4Health

Games4Health is another student innovation competition offered by The Sorenson Center for Discovery and Innovation, David Eccles School of Business at the University. It holds an annual competition ending in the spring with a capstone gala and award event. Starting in 2014, the competition has grown to include 14 countries and 85 international universities in 2017. Students can create wireframe games, share their ideas, and create promotional videos to enter the competition. The competition has gone from being a local one to an international one and now includes high school students who won three awards in the 2017 competition. Games are often themed around funding sponsor interests such as positive psychology. e-channel has collected this competition's outputs so they are organized, preserved, searchable, and therefore discoverable to many.

Technology Venture Commercialization

The UU TVC is tasked with helping UU faculty, staff, and students with taking mature ideas to the market. TVC offers consulting services, workshops, an incubator, and other services to entrepreneurs, including industry. They also sponsor a bimonthly event called Tech Tuesday to give UU and industry members a chance to learn about new products, programs, and opportunities and to network. The EHSL was a first co-sponsor of a Tech Tuesday when *Crossing the Chasm's* one author, Michael Eckhardt, was a speaker. This event's presentation and related materials are available on e-channel.

Working with the TVC, the EHSL faculty soon realized while there was a lot of information about innovation and entrepreneurship throughout the UU Innovation Ecosystem[5] websites, there was no one place where this information was readily available. The EHSL worked with TVC to generate an Innovation Lifecycle pointing to relevant UU resources pertinent to each stage of the innovation progress. This Innovation Lifecycle is on e-channel.

Imagine Perfect Care

Another UU Health program initiated by Dr. Lee was Imagine Perfect Care (IPC). IPC was started to encourage UU personnel to think of their efforts through the lens of a patient. Placing the patient at the center of health care creates a culture appreciated by patients and engages them to maximize their health care. IPC created a physical Resource Center bringing together in one space an environment where UU personnel can learn about others' initiatives and can test new concepts such as "room of the future." Several patient room mock-ups enabled staff to test workflows and efficient layouts of furniture and facilities. White Styrofoam walls outlining the room spaces enabled staff to write their ideas for changes right on the walls. The Resource Center showcased many EHSL initiatives such as an app bar (U-Bar), an Ideation Studio, a repository of patient education documents, and Healthi4U, a student-driven health video production competition. In return, EHSL promoted outputs from IPC Resource Center Open Houses and co-produced videos to illustrate IPC seed-funded accomplishments.

Department of Biomedical Informatics

The UU School of Medicine's Department of Biomedical Informatics (BMI) often sponsors lectures and visiting scholar events. The EHSL videotapes these occasions and includes them on e-channel when permission is gained from the speakers. BMI offers a Data Science for Health summer course to University personnel with EHSL providing technical support. Guest speaker video lectures are recorded and posted to e-channel each year the course is offered.

Moran Eye Center

The John A. Moran Eye Center is one of the premier research and clinical care eye centers in the United States. With a strong commitment to education and quality training for ophthalmologists both locally and internationally, the Moran Eye Center undertook an ambitious project to capture the work of its faculty, residents, and fellows with the goal of making hundreds of locally performed ophthalmic surgeries, unique case presentations, and lectures given by recognized experts freely available to the global ophthalmology community. The content creation was easily achieved, but the Moran Eye Center found itself challenged by the task of needing to organize, describe, and disseminate the content in a systematic way. After reaching out to EHSL for guidance, the two entities formed a collaboration to create the Moran Clinical Ophthalmology Resources for Education (CORE).[6] Working in partnership with eye center faculty, an organizational structure for presenting the material was developed and refined to accommodate variations in local and global training programs. Various content sources were identified and collection procedures established to capture those outputs. As content is produced, EHSL manages the process for submission, peer review, acceptance, and dissemination via the CORE, a component of e-channel.

While still in its early stages, this project has been a highly successful EHSL—Moran Center collaboration. Libraries are uniquely positioned to assist institutional departments to collect, organize, and disseminate their intellectual output via meaningful digital educational repositories.

Global Health

The UU has a history of global health initiatives addressing the systems and processes by which health care is delivered to patients around the world. Many University initiatives in this arena focus on potential changes to increase access, quality, and equitability. In pursuit of this goal, the institution has invited medical practitioners, policymakers, professionals, investors, technologists, students, and businesses to participate in an annual Extreme Affordability Conference[7] devoted to creatively tackling the challenges of accessible and affordable health care on a global scale.

The EHSL works collaboratively with the UU Global Health program to capture the innovative ideas and solutions shared at the conference. Interested parties who are unable to attend the Extreme Affordability Conference can visit e-channel to browse the collection of posters presented during the meeting. By partnering with Global Health to preserve and disseminate the output of this important endeavor, EHSL enables health-care practitioners to explore pilot programs already underway and identify the resources and professional connections needed to engage in future global health initiatives.

Healthi4U

Annually, the EHSL partners with other UU units to offer a student health video competition called Healthi4U to encourage students across all professions to create short videos to communicate health messages on a plentitude of topics.[8] Teams comprise three to five students from at least three disciplines. Five scholarship awards are granted to winning teams and resulting videos are shared via e-channel and selected ones via the UU Health Hospital's patient education television station.

Eccles Health Sciences Library

EHSL also places many of its activities and events in e-channel. Annually, EHSL holds an InfoFair to highlight the lightest technologies, related issues, key relevant topics, etc. Posters, videos, programs, etc., from these events are hosted on e-channel. The 2017 EHSL InfoFair was on the hot topic of research reproducibility. EHSL received grant funding several times to generate an awareness of sex and gender differences in research. Items produced by these grants are hosted in e-channel, including videos with underrepresented communities within the Salt Lake region documenting women's preferences for health care.

Additional Local Partner Links

There are several additional partners included in e-channel where contributed content is not stored within the WordPress platform but linked to the content to highlight it. The reasoning for this is because of the amount of storage and labor required to duplicate the content. Examples of these include the ARUP Institute for Learning,[9] creating educational modules to enhance medical laboratory practice throughout the country, and the Scope radio show, producing daily podcasts and health instructional content.[10] In time, it is hoped some of the content displayed by these e-channel tiles can be added to the e-channel platform for preservation purposes.

CONTENT COLLABORATIONS: NATIONAL PARTNERSHIP—VENTUREWELL

Attendance at different gaming and innovation conferences led to the former director of the EHSL contacting the professional association staff sponsoring such conferences to determine interest in sharing content with e-channel. One association agreeing to contribute conference output to e-channel was the National Collegiate Inventors and Innovators Alliance (NCIIA), now VentureWell. Through conversations with NCIIA staff, pdf versions of contributed posters have been added to e-channel since 2014. Posters are not exclusively on e-channel, but are preserved there as VentureWell replaces their conference posters annually on their site.

CONTENT COLLABORATIONS: INTERNATIONAL PARTNERSHIPS

Innovation Vault

The field of innovation and entrepreneurship education has been growing rapidly at universities throughout the world. The UU has joined numerous peer institutions in devoting resources supporting the curriculum needs of this discipline. To broaden the field of content experts from whom students can learn, EHSL partnered with the Canadian Innovation Centre (CIC) to create the Innovation Vault on e-channel.

CIC is a national, not-for-profit organization dedicated to helping innovators, inventors, and entrepreneurs transform their ideas into market successes. In 2012, Andrew Maxwell, the CIO and Director of Partner Relations at CIC, began capturing video interviews with luminaries in the field of innovation and entrepreneurship with the goal of creating a resource of current industry and academic knowledge. As the project grew, he also began collecting video documentation of lectures, seminars, and conference breakout sessions on topics relevant to the field. The challenge then was to organize these hundreds of videos into a searchable database offering ease of access and topical discoverability. Discussions between the CIC and EHSL led both parties to conclude that the organizational expertise of EHSL could solve this dilemma and a project partnership was quickly established.

The CIC agreed to provide the video content to EHSL for inclusion on e-channel, while EHSL agreed to curate, describe, organize, and preserve the collection in a way optimizing its discoverability and usefulness for academic programs devoted to innovation and entrepreneurship. The resulting Innovation Vault is a rich video library enhancing learning by exposing viewers to insights and best practices developed by industry leaders. More information about the Innovation Vault and e-channel itself may be found in the book, *Information and Innovation: A Natural Combination for Health Sciences Libraries.*[11]

Digital Games Research Association

Another international professional association partnering with EHSL by contributing content to e-channel was DiGRA—Digital Games Research Association. Their president happened to be a faculty of The GApp Lab at the UU, and thus connections were easy to make as the Lab had helped to create e-channel's first platform. He shared the idea with the governing board of DiGRA who readily agreed. Annual meeting presentations and posters for the last 3 years are available via e-channel and DiGRA's website.

LESSONS LEARNED

Producing e-channel has led to many lessons learned from technological perspectives to philosophical and cultural differences. EHSL staff were given a chance to redirect skills required by a print library environment to an online digital collection format through the creation of e-channel.

Additional skills were needed such as graphic arts, WordPress management, and marketing talent.

Culturally, one main lesson learned is innovators are not as willing to share content as other kinds of academic personnel as a result of the commercialization future for their output. Ideas, even failed ones, are of great value. While they may not spark at one moment in time, with later innovations or a fresh set of eyes, a failed idea can turn into a gem of one with the right cultivation and growth environment. Originally it was envisioned innovative teams would be willing to complete structured templates to document their contributions, their progress, and the barriers to success; this has not proven to be the case. Students find it difficult to complete even competition-related paperwork with their time constraints, let alone complete an "achievement" document. Intellectual property rights mean more than just promotion or tenure potential with innovators—it can translate into real dollars and revenue for not only them but their associated institutions as well.

As with most things in life, finding the sweet moment when someone has a need you can fulfill or address is when e-channel comes to the rescue. Personnel need to reach a pain point before they will take the time to add content and contribute to e-channel. A champion also can assist with encouraging peers and others to think about preserving their output via e-channel.

Creating a platform such as e-channel dependent upon the submission of content from others takes patience and time to develop. Individuals need to be able to understand the value they will gain from contributing their output to such a venue without a recognizable brand or broad awareness. Understanding how easy contributing to e-channel is seemed to be another hurdle. A comment statement was "I don't know how to submit my contributions so I haven't." Getting word about e-channel out across the University has been a challenge as there are so many different scholarly communication venues available to University personnel. Being able to decipher which ones add value to busy workloads has been an issue. The tipping point for selling e-channel has been its preservation nature. While each innovative group has desired to keep its current content on its local website or media outlet, knowing content will be accurately described and preserved by e-channel has offered the release of a lot of output to e-channel. Gaining the trust of innovators has been a key achievement. Building relationships over time to gain trust has been invaluable.

While failure reporting was encouraged, very few have been submitted. Is the word "failure" too harsh? Does a failure often lead to a commercializable success and therefore should be protected and not shared with others? Innovators are encouraged to fail hard and often—it is a culture norm—meant to be iterative and therefore, perhaps not documented? Time will tell.

FUTURE COLLABORATIONS

With the value of intellectual property in mind, a future goal for e-channel is to work with the UU Health Faculty Affairs office to see if academic credit can be granted to items hosted by e-channel, especially if a peer review process can be initiated for content acceptance. Altmetric impact can be gained for such items as they are multimedia and openly available via the Internet. If e-channel is recognized locally and nationally as the one key source for innovation-related information, inclusion of faculty content will enhance individual academic portfolios for promotion and tenure.

More content from a variety of sources will be added to e-channel soon. Additional global health content and output from the UU's quality units will be forthcoming. As new videos and company stories are created by Lassonde Entrepreneur Institute[12] participants as part of its *Launch* program, they will be described and posted on e-channel. Content originating from the University's Entrepreneurial Faculty Scholars (EFS) various programs is being culled. The addition of EFS means all the UU Innovation Ecosystem units have employed e-channel as their official archival site,[5] and thus a link to e-channel has been added to the Ecosystem's website. As the student competitions described in this chapter hold their annual events, resulting output will be posted. Other innovation-related professional associations are being contacted to see if they are willing to share any content they generate. As more people get comfortable with reporting their failures, e-channel can be the source for disseminating them as well.

SUMMARY

All in all, e-channel has been a successful initiative for the EHSL. While most of the current content derives from individuals associated with the University, there is starting to be uptake from national associations and others. It has enabled library staff to transition their skills from print collections to digital ones, and it has served to document knowledge being generated by the University's innovators. It has also assisted EHSL with building key collaborations and partners with several internal University units and external national and international agencies. A one-stop-shop for innovation-related information, educational programs, and self-guided development, e-channel welcomes anyone to submit content by contacting the lead author of this book chapter.

REFERENCES

1. *e-channel*. Salt Lake City, UT: Spencer S. Eccles Health Sciences Library; 2017, 2014–2017. Available from: http://library.med.utah.edu/e-channel/.
2. Jarvis C, Gregory JM, Shipman JP. Books to bytes at the speed of light: a rapid health sciences collection transformation. *Collect Manag*. 2014;39(2–3):60–76. https://doi.org/10.1080/01462679.2014.910150.
3. *The GApp Lab*. Salt Lake City, UT: Therapeutic Games & Apps Lab; 2016. Available from: http://thegapp.eae.utah.edu/.
4. e-channel. *The GApp Lab Wrap Kits*. Salt Lake City, UT: Spencer S. Eccles Health Sciences Library; 2017, 2014–2017. Available from: http://library.med.utah.edu/e-channel/portfolio/gapp-lab-wrap-kits/.
5. The University of Utah. *Welcome to the Innovation Ecosystem*. Salt Lake City, UT: University of Utah; 2017. Available from: http://www.utah.edu/innovate.
6. e-channel. *Moran CORE*. Salt Lake City, UT: Spencer S. Eccles Health Sciences Library; 2017, 2014–2017. Available from: https://library.med.utah.edu/e-channel/portfolio/moran-core-clinical-ophthalmology-resources-for-education/.
7. University of Utah Global Health. *Global Health Extreme Affordability Conference*. Salt Lake City, UT: University of Utah; 2017. Available from: http://uofuhealth.utah.edu/globalhealth/extreme-affordability.
8. Spencer S. Eccles Health Sciences Library. *Healthi4U*. Salt Lake City, UT: Spencer S. Eccles Health Sciences Library; 2017, 1993–2017. Available from: https://library.med.utah.edu/e-channel/portfolio/healthi4u/.
9. e-channel. *ARUP Lab Education*. Salt Lake City, UT: Spencer S. Eccles Health Sciences Library; 2017, 2014–2017. Available from: https://library.med.utah.edu/e-channel/portfolio/arup-lab-education/.
10. e-channel. *The Scope – University of Utah Health Sciences Radio*. Salt Lake City, UT: Spencer S. Eccles Health Sciences Library; 2017, 2014–2017. Available from: https://library.med.utah.edu/e-channel/portfolio/the-scope-university-of-utah-health-sciences-radio/.
11. Shipman JP, Ulmer BA, eds. *Information and Innovation: A Natural Combination for Health Sciences Libraries*. Lanham, MD: Rowman & Littlefield; 2017, 194 p.
12. University of Utah Lassonde Entrepreneur Institute. *Lassonde Entrepreneur Institute*. Salt Lake City, UT: University of Utah; 2017. Available from: http://lassonde.utah.edu.

CHAPTER 10

It Takes a Village: Operating an App Bar Within a Hospital

Erica Lake[1], John Christian Tueller Bramble[2], Heidi Greenberg[1], Jean P. Shipman[1,3] Robin L. Marcus[4,5] Chris Lyle Wasden[6], Kyle Bradford Jones[7]
[1]Spencer S. Eccles Health Sciences Library, University of Utah, Salt Lake City, UT, United States; [2]National Network of Libraries of Medicine MidContinental Region, Spencer S. Eccles Health Sciences Library, University of Utah, Salt Lake City, UT, United States; [3]Global Library Relations, GSN, Elsevier, Cottonwood Heights, UT, United States; [4]Department of Physical Therapy and Athletic Training, University of Utah, Salt Lake City, UT, United States; [5]Office of Wellness and Integrative Health, University of Utah Health, Salt Lake City, UT, United States; [6]Managing Partner of Digital Disruption Advisors, Midway, UT, United States; [7]Family and Preventive Medicine, University of Utah School of Medicine, Salt Lake City, UT, United States

BACKGROUND

Rise of Digital Health Technologies

Americans daily touch their smartphones over 2600 times, use them over 145 min, and engage them for 76 separate phone sessions.[1] They use them for nearly everything—smartphones are transforming the way they feel, think, and act. According to a recent Pew Research Study survey, roughly three-quarters of Americans (77%) now own a smartphone, with lower-income Americans and those aged 50 and older exhibiting a sharp uptick in ownership between 2014 and 2016.[2] More than 40% of those over age 65 own a smartphone as of this writing. Nearly 7 out of 10 Americans use social media, and half the public own a tablet computer.[2] Though less widespread than smartphones, tablet computers have also become highly common in a very short period of time, increasing access to the Internet for a wide range of individuals.

People use digital technologies to stay connected to friends and family, to check email, track productivity, and for entertainment. According to a 2015 New York University study, 58% of smartphone users have downloaded a digital health and fitness app.[3] Individuals can easily record the number of daily steps, calories consumed, or specific health metrics like blood glucose, blood pressure, and body weight. There are apps reminding people to take medications, fill prescriptions and communicate with health-care providers. Digital technology is radically transforming all aspects of American culture, and health care is no exception.

Strategic Collaborations in Health Sciences Libraries
ISBN 978-0-08-102258-0
https://doi.org/10.1016/B978-0-08-102258-0.00010-0
Copyright © 2019 Jean P. Shipman and M.J. Tooey. Published by Elsevier Limited. All rights reserved.

Patients Interested in Digital Health Technologies

According to the "2015 State of the Connected Patient" survey by Sales Force, 63% of millennials indicated interest in proactively monitoring their health and well-being, and 71% indicated interest in their doctor recommending apps.[4] International Data Corporation, the world's leading technology media, events, and research company, predicts 65% of consumer transactions with health-care organizations will be mobile by 2018, as a response to consumer desires to improve the patient experience.[5] To help control health-care costs in this same timeframe—especially for patients with chronic conditions—they suggest that 70% of health-care organizations worldwide will invest in consumer-facing apps, wearable devices, remote health monitoring, and virtual care. Consistent with the rise in consumer interest in digital health technologies, pharmaceutical companies, health-care providers, payers, and administrators are looking to digital solutions to engage patients in preventive health and well-being behaviors and in managing chronic disease and moving patients toward healthier practices.[6]

Health-Care Providers and Administrators Interested in Digital Health Technologies

While numerous studies[7] have been done on various digital health diagnostics and therapeutics demonstrating improved access to care, lower costs, and improved outcomes, there appear to be an equal number questioning the value of digital health technologies to make a difference in the practice of medicine and patient benefit.[8] Therefore, the impact of digital health technologies on patient health outcomes remains elusive; however, based upon the transformative impact digital technologies have had in all other aspects of living, it appears the potential to improve patient outcomes, lower health-care costs, and motivate and encourage patient engagement and activation should be able to become a reality.[9] A recent *NEJM Catalyst* Insight Council survey reported the top two benefits of using digital health technology for patient engagement included supporting patients in their efforts to be healthy and providing input to providers on how patients are doing when not in the clinic. With respect to engaging patients in their own care, apps were identified as effective, very effective, or extremely effective by 75% of survey respondents.[10] Wearable devices and wireless biometric sensors were also highlighted as effective digital health technologies for this purpose.

Challenge

The rise in digital health technologies and the infrastructure to support their use, combined with patient and health-care provider interest, presents an unprecedented opportunity to test the impact of digital health technologies in supporting patient health behaviors and outcomes. More than 325,000 digital health apps were available as of 2017, and most lack clinical and economic evidence of their effectiveness.[11] The challenge now is determining how to ensure efficacy and safety for patients wishing to engage in digital health technology. The United States Food and Drug Administration (FDA) has stated they believe they do not need to regulate the vast majority of digital health apps because they merely provide information and tracking tools, and address areas of fitness and wellness.[12] The FDA believes it only needs to regulate those digital health apps meeting one or more of the following three criteria: (1) are a companion digital solution to an existing FDA-regulated therapy or medical device; (2) replace a clinician or health-care professional; and (3) diagnose a medical condition.[12] With few health-care professionals involved in the development of most digital health apps, and with no consensus on how to evaluate and recommend apps to patients, consumers are left to fend for themselves. Dr. James Madara, chief executive officer of the American Medical Association (AMA), during the 2016 Annual AMA Meeting, referring to the current landscape of medical information technology innovation, lamented a lack of involvement from the medical establishment. Madera recommended medical professional societies directly create initiatives to help patients find and understand content on apps.[13] To that end, the AMA has partnered with industry leaders and innovators to promote the Xcertia guidelines for digital health app development and management.[14]

In response, the University of Utah (University) wanted to address these challenges and become an early adopter and national leader in providing a patient and consumer digital health formulary that would work much like a pharmaceutical formulary does today—to help guide physicians in prescribing medications. This formulary became a means to achieve three goals: (1) connect University Health's efforts toward improved patient experiences and increased focus on preventive health and wellness, (2) improve the University Health Plans outreach efforts, and (3) enhance the University's reputation for innovation.

CREATION OF THE U-BAR

The U-Bar was a true collaboration—envisioned, developed, and created by a village of individuals from across the University. The founding members of the U-Bar Team included the chief wellness officer, a director from University of Utah Health Plans, the executive director for the Center for Medical Innovation, and the executive director for the Discovery and Innovation Center at the University's School of Business.

University health sciences librarians were invited to participate on the Team, including the executive director of the Spencer S. Eccles Health Sciences Library (EHSL), associate director of the Hope Fox Eccles Health Library (Library), and additional EHSL faculty and staff. Rounding out the representation on the Team were clinicians, informatics faculty, health games and apps faculty, marketing and communications staff, hospital information technology staff, and hospital facilities and design staff.

The Team began to discuss what the U-Bar might look like and what policies and procedures would be needed to operate it. Labor was divided as appropriate. No one formally chaired the Team, although the EHSL coordinated meetings and provided extensive project oversight.

Inspiration

The Team's inspiration came from the Apple Genius Bar, where consumers can, at no cost, get help and support in using their digital devices. They saw how other organizations had created a similar model to guide patients, consumers, and clinicians to understand, identify, select, and use health apps and wearable devices to improve their health-care experience. These included Oschner Health System's O-Bar[15] and Morristown Medical Center's Health*e*Connect Store.[16]

Goal

The goal was to create a highly visible, active digital health technologies hub where patients, visitors, consumers, and clinicians could test-drive vetted apps on demo tablets, look at and acquire various wearable devices, and share information and experiences in a welcoming environment.

Branding

The Team decided to call the service the U-Bar to reflect the familiarity of individuals with Apple's Genius Bars and align with the O-Bar name adopted by the Oschner Health System. Initially, the "U" reinforced the familiarity of the University location. No logo or identifiable visual element was created initially.

Funding

The executive director of the Center for Medical Innovation met with the Hospital CEO to inquire about funding a beta launch of the service. $50,000 was provided for start-up funds, and the money was divided between the Hospital, to cover physical construction and equipment, and the College of Health, to cover part-time student staff.

Location and Remodel

The Hospital CEO determined the initial placement of the U-Bar would be within the entrance area of the Library, the consumer health library located just off the Hospital's lobby. As the main thoroughfare for the Hospital, thousands of visitors pass through the lobby daily, and it is where the Gift Shop, Pharmacy, and Starbucks are also located. He did not agree to place it at a more visible Information Desk within the lobby itself so as not to impede the traffic flow.

The Hospital facility designer created a mock-up of how the Library space could be remodeled to accommodate the U-Bar equipment and staff. As the location was intended to be temporary for a beta launch, a streamlined, mobile design was favored over built-in fixtures and furnishings.

Equipment

The U-Bar was equipped with four Apple iPad Air 2 tablets with 32 GB. Two of the iPads were inserted into secured, free-standing pedestals from IdeaCom, and the other two iPads served as backup devices. Hospital information technology staff manually installed the vetted apps (explained below) on each iPad and used MobileIron, a security tool for wireless devices, to filter content to avoid abuse and control downloads. An LG Smart TV with WebOS2.0, a Tru-4k Engine, and a 43″ monitor was used to display what appeared on either iPad. U-Bar staff could use it for health app consultations, trainings, or demonstrations for patients, visitors, and hospital staff. This equipment can be seen in Fig. 10.1.

Building the Vetted App Collection

The U-Bar Team determined the initial collection of apps and wearable devices should address the top 10 diagnoses identified by the University Health Plans. As a result, the apps primarily focused on common health issues known to contribute positively to overall health, such as weight

Figure 10.1 The U-Bar.

loss and physical activity. A few specialized resources were added to address glucose monitoring, asthma management, and prenatal health tracking.

While there was a discussion about the need for formal evaluation criteria and a selection process, neither was implemented. Instead, several U-Bar Team members with digital health technology expertise guided the initial selection process, and different Hospital teams were asked to provide their recommended apps. The Team decided the collection should comprise apps currently available and popular in the marketplace, with documented efficacy and low risk, available in iOS and Android versions, and free. Using these initial criteria, 16 apps and 3 wearable devices were selected. These apps and wearables are highlighted in Table 10.1.

Management, Staffing, and Training

Personnel management and supervision of the U-Bar staff fell to the chief wellness officer, who recruited paid students from the University's College of Health. Initially, five students were hired to provide coverage during U-Bar business hours, which were 8 a.m. to 5 p.m., Monday through Friday.

The undergraduate and graduate students were trained by College of Health supervisors to provide one-on-one assistance to visitors on installing and using the U-Bar apps and wearable devices. The students downloaded each app on their personal phone or tablet, and used them for a week. They

Table 10.1 The initial collection of U-Barvetted apps and wearable devices

App name
Air Now
Glucose Buddy
iTriage
Lose It!
Map My Hike
Map My Ride
Map My Run
Migraine Buddy
MyChart
My Fitness Pal
mySugr
One Drop
Ovia Pregnancy
Spark People
Strava
WellnessNOW
Wearable name
FitBit
Withings Health Mate
Microsoft Health

also rotated through the various wearable devices so they could learn the nuances and strengths of each kind. With this hands-on training, the students became able to aid technology-savvy visitors seeking recommendations comparing similar tools, and also those who were new to these technologies and needed step-by-step guidance.

The staff also received consumer health training from librarians on the various diseases and conditions addressed by the apps, such as diabetes, to better understand the significance of having an app to monitor glucose levels. In addition, the librarians provided training on how to assist Library users with more general questions, and the students attended the new employee Hospital orientation.

Publicity

The Team worked with University Health Marketing and Communications to publicize the opening of the U-Bar and describe the services available. Marketing and Communications developed posters and flyers to display throughout the Hospital, a table tent announcement to place in the

Hospital cafeteria and clinics, and published an announcement on the internal intranet news site to reach employees. In addition, members of the U-Bar Team visited with leadership groups throughout the organization to introduce the service and provided demonstrations at internal open-house events, and a local do-it-yourself festival and a community health fair.

Marketing and Communications created a web version of the U-Bar on the Library website.[17] The vetted apps were listed on this site and made available for downloading remotely. This expanded the reach of the U-Bar, allowing patients in clinics located throughout the city to have online access to the app collection.

Many of the selected apps required wearable devices to collect relevant biometric data. To ensure having access to such devices was not a barrier for patients and caregivers, an agreement with the Hospital Gift Shop was reached for it to carry and sell the most popular devices. The shop's manager arranged a plan with the nearby University health sciences bookstore to be able to quickly replenish supplies and to offer even more options to users.

Metrics

No patient health data were collected, and none of the vetted apps or wearables were formally synched to electronic health records (EHRs) or the patient portal. Instead, U-Bar students collected information on the service at every visitor encounter using a Google Form loaded on a staff iPad. The information included how visitors were referred to the U-Bar, the name of the referring provider, what apps they were interested in, what apps they downloaded, and the phone or tablet type used for the download. A satisfaction survey was also given to each visitor to appraise the usefulness of the information they received and to get suggestions for improvements. Additional metrics captured the app download activity on the U-Bar webpage. After the first 2 months of the beta launch, the U-Bar had a total of 40 visitors. Four of those were the result of physician referrals. Fifty-six percent found the U-Bar very useful; 44% found it somewhat useful, while 100% found the students very helpful.

CONCLUSIONS

Launching the U-Bar as a beta service allowed for flexibility as it morphed and grew. U-Bar Team members identified key strengths and weaknesses and worked to address these to foster broader implementation of the program.

A second round of funding was obtained from Hospital administration to support continuation of the service, covering operational student and staff costs, and some promotion and marketing costs. A Memorandum of Agreement was written between Hospital administration, the chief wellness officer, and the executive director of the EHSL. It set expectations for student training and the collection of performance metrics. It also established an EHSL-dedicated staff to oversee the U-Bar Team, manage promotion and marketing efforts, and prepare midyear and annual status reports. The Memorandum of Agreement will be renewed annually, based upon acceptable performance and available funding.

Formal Evaluation and Selection Criteria

One common feedback from providers surrounded the trustworthiness of the vetted app collection. Having a formal evaluation and selection process ensured provider confidence in recommending the apps to patients and was a crucial requirement for future success. The Team initially lacked the manpower to develop and sustain a vetting process, and at one point explored licensing a third-party company to do this work. EHSL faculty then formed a subcommittee to do the vetting, comprising clinical and technology experts and the U-Bar students.

Few validated, standardized protocols for the objective evaluation and rating of health apps existed at the time; namely the Mobile App Rating Scale (MARS),[18] and uMARS[19]—the simplified version of MARS created for user evaluation projects and effectiveness trials. The U-Bar evaluation subcommittee modified and expanded uMARS to incorporate safety, security, and privacy criteria; implemented its use; and plans to conduct studies to validate it.

Refine, Grow, and Bundle Vetted Apps to Address Specific Diseases/Conditions

One of the biggest challenges with the use of health apps is the continued growth and evolution of those offered. Not only did the number of health-related apps increase by 57% in 2016 when compared to 2015,[20] but many of them included new options in both number and efficacy.

Addressing this meant expanding and refining the vetted collection of U-Bar apps in a focused and strategic way. The vetting went beyond the most popular apps, and bundles were created addressing a given disease from multiple angles. For example, multiple technologies assisting patients with diabetes can assist with glucose control, blood pressure management, weight loss, carbohydrate counting, and other dietary measures, etc. Apps addressing the many social determinants of health, such as finding bus routes to get to the clinic, finding the best deals on healthy food at local grocery stores, or help in finding affordable and clean housing options in safe neighborhoods, were also bundled. Subject experts from the U-Bar Team and invited clinicians and health-care professionals, assisted in developing these app bundles.

Educate Health-Care Providers on Apps' Impact on Patient Health

A significant barrier to more widespread use of the U-Bar was provider knowledge about the options available and education on incorporating the use of digital health technologies into regular clinical practice and research. Many providers receive inquiries from patients about various apps, but have little experience with knowing which ones to recommend. Providers who receive education on the uses of digital health technologies in improving health, are potentially more equipped to champion and promote U-Bar and app prescriptions to their peers. This education can be accomplished through presentations at Grand Rounds, written articles, webinars, or other forms of continuing medical education.

Research Applications

The U-Bar can serve as a collection point to register potential participants in digital health technology research, contributing to the body of clinical and economic evidence on effectiveness of health apps. Team members have publicized this opportunity to the local research community. One example was a partnership between the U-Bar and the Utah Center for Excellence in ELSI (Ethical, Legal and Social Implications) Research (UCEER). UCEER's T3 translational research proposal involved newborn screening and dried bloodspot education implementation, coupled with novel electronic research methods.

Integration Into Electronic and Personal Health Records

Possibly the biggest barrier to broader adoption of apps by health-care system personnel is the lack of a convenient way for information to be included in individuals' health records. Health-care providers are more inclined to integrate patient-generated health data (PGHD) in decision-making if it is included in EHRs.[21] While some of these applications can currently be added to the health record, many cannot. The process of connecting data from the apps to medical records is time consuming and onerous. Working with the medical record vendors is essential for ease of uploading and maintaining patient data.

Food and Drug Administration Approval of Health Technology Devices

An increase in PGHD contributes to patient empowerment about their health and improved clinical decision-making with health-care providers.[22] The 21st Century Cures Act, passed in 2016, includes multiple provisions supporting innovative wearable and digital health technologies, and clarifies the FDA's role in medical software and technological regulation.[23] The impact of this law means many app technologies will not need full FDA approval; however, the efficacy and safety of many wearable technologies will still be subject to FDA scrutiny, especially those impacting patient privacy.[24] This includes devices assisting with anything from glucose monitoring to detecting an oncoming seizure before it occurs. As regulation of these devices changes, approval may become more streamlined, and the number of technologies may increase. Increased availability of externally vetted and approved apps and technologies will contribute to the increased success of the U-Bar service.

Further Utilize University Innovations

The University has other programs to further the utilization and expanse of the U-Bar. THEerapeutic Games and Apps Lab—The GApp Lab—is a collaboration between the Center for Medical Innovation, the Entertainment Arts and Engineering program, and the EHSL where University students create therapeutic, medical, academic, and educational video games, mobile apps, and websites for both internal and external clients. Many of the creations address how to assist patients with gaining a better understanding of their health to increase their well-being, often having a therapeutic component designed to work in conjunction with other treatment modalities. Current examples include games educating and supporting personal habits for the management of Type II diabetes, an augmented reality platform assisting in relieving phantom limb pain in individuals with amputations, and a game encouraging medication compliance.

The University's Sorenson Center for Discovery & Innovation hosts an annual Games4Health, a student health game design competition. Participants are invited from across the globe. They compete for monetary prizes for innovative and efficacious health game creations. As the U-Bar expands, further collaboration with these University entities could improve the options and tools available.

ROLE OF HEALTH SCIENCES LIBRARIANS

One of only a handful of hospital consumer app services in the nation, the U-Bar is the only service with health sciences librarian involvement. Librarians performed a wide variety of tasks in developing this service and demonstrated to others how they could apply their expertise and contribute their skills and knowledge in nontraditional ways.

Project Design

The associate director of the Library drafted the initial service proposal, and the EHSL executive director presented it to the U-Bar Team for review and to the Hospital CEO and clinic administration for approval and funding. The proposal included a business plan with a budget overview and narrative and provided information related to the U-Bar management, publicity, and performance metrics. Developing a proposal with this level of detail showed librarians had the necessary knowledge to oversee a digital health project.

Project Management

The coordination and management of this project required a large effort of time and knowledge. As mentioned, no one formally chaired the U-Bar Team; however, the librarian team members provided most of the project management. The librarians interacted with a broad cross section of individuals, from Hospital executives to clinicians, to connect the right people to the project meeting skill and resource needs.

Roughly 6 months into the project, one librarian on the Team was funded at 20% to provide oversight. This included convening different meetings, coordinating Team efforts (including app installation), collecting and analyzing performance metrics, preparing midyear and annual status reports, and overseeing marketing and promotion efforts. Upon seeking continuation funding, a formal Memorandum of Understanding (MOU) was created with Hospital administration, acknowledging a librarian as the U-Bar's project manager.

Business

Business skills utilized included creating concept proposals, an MOU, budget proposals and management, and cost accounting associated with construction of the U-Bar. Marketing skills were also needed to work with the marketing unit to create materials to advertise and educate consumers about U-Bar offerings. Meeting management skills included scheduling meeting, agenda planning, implementing Team decisions and ideas, and monitoring of action plans.

Evaluation

Consumer health librarians strive to ensure patients and their family members have access to timely, quality health information to aid better decision-making and to achieve behavioral change and disease management goals. Digital technology resources can be a source of such information, just like books and journals, and librarians are skilled at connecting people to quality information, regardless of the medium.

Determining the quality of information is a long-standing skill possessed by librarians. Evaluating the quality of apps aligns perfectly within the realm of librarians' capabilities. An important part of the app evaluation process was collaboration with subject specialists, such as clinicians, who contributed their expertise on content and appropriateness for use by various patient populations.

Librarians led the development of a systematic health app evaluation based on key quality information measures found in published research. They also developed a workflow mechanism assigning experts to evaluate app features within their domains, and guided them throughout the process of completing app evaluations.

Training

Librarians utilized instruction skills to offer training to clinicians, other health-care professionals, and students on digital health technologies. Training was delivered in a variety of ways, including scheduled consultations, departmental training, videos, printed materials, and website resources. The librarians also participated in the EHSL *Appy Hour* series—an educational hour devoted to digital health technologies—to showcase U-Bar apps and encourage providers to refer patients to these apps.

Librarians developed additional training for U-Bar staff on how to search Johns Hopkins University's online reference of aggregate studies—mHealth Evidence[25]—and other online databases for literature and clinical trials demonstrating the feasibility, usability, and efficacy of health apps.

Knowledge of EHRs

Being familiar with EHRs, and provider workflows within EHRs, allowed librarians to oversee the creation of a new order entry for referral to the U-Bar. A process was implemented for providers to prescribe such referrals within the local EHR. The referral includes the "prescribed" app (e.g., a glucose monitor) or type of app (e.g., an activity tracker) and provides details on how to obtain assistance with the app at the U-Bar. The referrals are taken by patients to the U-Bar for fulfillment by the Library staff.

Promotion

The librarian U-Bar Team members presented ideas and project findings at national and regional professional conferences via presentations and posters. Librarians also established a Twitter feed—#ubarapps—to publicize newly published research and clinical trials incorporating health apps and wearable devices and to share digital health technology industry news.

WHY LIBRARIANS?

Because most libraries serve a broad array of constituents, librarians tend to work across institutions and communities, making connections and bringing the right people to an issue. Librarians were valuable collaborators on the U-bar Team precisely because of this attribute.

Librarians are adopting new roles and incorporating technology in new ways to meet the needs of patients, caregivers, clinicians, faculty, and students.[26] Tremendous opportunities exist in digital health to strengthen and broaden clinical and campus professional relationships to contribute to innovative services and resources. Many patients desire "high-tech" health services coupled with "high-touch" interactions.[27] The U-Bar app service is one example of a creative way librarians connect patients to critical health information and tools, increasing their engagement and satisfaction, and ultimately, improving health outcomes.

REFERENCES

1. *Mobile Touches: Dscout's Inaugural Study on Humans and Their Tech*; 2016. Available from: http://blog.dscout.com/hubfs/downloads/dscout_mobile_touches_study_2016.pdf.
2. Smith A. *Record Shares of Americans Now Own Smartphones, Have Home Broadband*; 2017. Available from: http://www.pewresearch.org/fact-tank/2017/01/12/evolution-of-technology/.

3. Krebs P, Duncan DT. Health app use among US mobile phone owners: A national survey. *JMIR Mhealth Uhealth*. 2015;3(4):e101. https://doi.org/10.2196/mhealth.4924.
4. Salesforce. *2015 State of the Connected Patient*; 2015. Available from: https://secure2.sfdcstatic.com/assets/pdf/industries/2015-State-of-the-Connected-Patient.pdf.
5. Gramling A. *10 predictions for Healthcare IT in 2015*; 2015. Available from: https://www.healthcareitleaders.com/blog/10-predictions-healthcare-2015/.
6. Sawesi S, Rashrash M, Phalakornkule K, Carpenter JS, Jones JF. The impact of information technology on patient engagement and health behavior change: a systematic review of the literature. Eysenbach G, ed. *JMIR Med Informat*. 2016;4(1):e1. https://doi.org/10.2196/medinform.4514.
7. Free C, Phillips G, Watson L, et al. The effectiveness of mobile-health technologies to improve health care service delivery processes: a systematic review and meta-analysis. Cornford T, ed. *PLoS Med*. 2013;10(1):e1001363. https://doi.org/10.1371/journal.pmed.1001363.
8. Goldzweig CL, Towfigh A, Maglione M, Shekelle PG. Costs and benefits of health information technology: new trends from the literature. *Health Aff (Millwood)*. March—April 2009;28(2):w282—w293. Epub 2009 Jan 27. https://doi.org/10.1377/hlthaff.28.2.w282.
9. O'Connor S, Hanlon P, O'Donnell CA, Garcia S, Glanville J, Mair FS. Understanding factors affecting patient and public engagement and recruitment to digital health interventions: a systematic review of qualitative studies. *BMC Med Inform Decis Mak*. September 15, 2016;16(1):120. https://doi.org/10.1186/s12911-016-0359-3.
10. Lee TH, Campion EW, Morrissey S, Drazen JM. Leading the transformation of health care delivery - the launch of NEJM catalyst. *N Engl J Med*. 2015;373:2468—2469. https://doi.org/10.1056/NEJMe1515517.
11. Research 2 Guidance. *325,000 Mobile Health Apps Available in 2017 — Android Now the Leading MHealth Platform*; 2017. Available from: https://research2guidance.com/325000-mobile-health-apps-available-in-2017/.
12. US Food and Drug Administration. *Digital Health*; 2018. Available from: https://www.fda.gov/medicaldevices/digitalhealth/.
13. American Medical Association. *AMA CEO Outlines Digital Challenges, Opportunities Facing Medicine*; 2016. Available from: https://www.ama-assn.org/ama-ceo-outlines-digital-challenges-opportunities-facing-medicine.
14. American Medical Association. *New Digital Health Innovations for Better Patient Care*; 2017. Available from: https://www.ama-assn.org/ama-digital-health-care-innovations.
15. *The O Bar*. New Orleans (LA): Ochsner Health System; 2018. Available from: https://www.ochsner.org/io/the-o-bar.
16. *HealtheConnect Store*. Morristown (NJ): Morristown Medical Center; 2018. Available from: https://www.atlantichealth.org/morristown/the-patient-experience/hospital-stays/healtheconnect-store.html.
17. *U-Bar Apps*. Salt Lake City (UT): University of Utah Health; 2017. Available from: https://healthcare.utah.edu/locations/hospital/library/u-bar-apps.php.
18. Stoyanov SR, Hides L, Kavanagh DJ, Zelenko O, Tjondronegoro D, Mani M. Mobile App Rating Scale: a new tool for assessing the quality of health mobile apps. Eysenbach G, ed. *JMIR mHealth and uHealth*. 2015;3(1):e27. https://doi.org/10.2196/mhealth.3422.
19. Stoyanov SR, Hides L, Kavanagh DJ, Wilson H. Development and validation of the user version of the mobile application rating Scale (uMARS). Eysenbach G, ed. *JMIR mHealth and uHealth*. 2016;4(2):e72. https://doi.org/10.2196/mhealth.5849.
20. *Research 2 Guidance. mHealth App Developer Economics 2016*; 2016. Available from: https://research2guidance.com/product/mhealth-app-developer-economics-2016/.

21. Cohen DJ, Keller SR, Hayes GR, Dorr DA, Ash J, Sittig DF. Integrating patient-generated health data into clinical care settings or clinical-decision making: lessons learned from project health design. *JMIR Hum Factors*. July—December 2016;3(2):e26. https://doi.org/10.2196/humanfactors.5919.
22. The Office of the National Coordinator for Health Information Technology. *Conceptualizing a Data Infrastructure for the Capture, Use, and Sharing of Patient-Generated Health Data in Care Delivery and Research through 2024*; 2018. Available from: https://www.healthit.gov/sites/default/files/onc_pghd_final_white_paper.pdf.
23. US Congress. *21st Century Cures Act, Pub. L. No. 114-255, 130 Stat. 1033*; 2016. Available from: https://www.congress.gov/bill/114th-congress/house-bill/34/text.
24. Federal Trade Commission. *Mobile Health Apps Interactive Tool*; 2016. Available from: https://www.ftc.gov/tips-advice/business-center/guidance/mobile-health-apps-interactive-tool.
25. *mHealth Evidence*. Baltimore (MD): Johns Hopkins; 2018. Available from: https://www.mhealthevidence.org/.
26. Henderson M. New roles and new horizons for health sciences librarians and libraries. In: Wood MS, ed. *Health Sciences Librarianship*. Chicago: Rowman & Littlefield and the Medical Library Association; 2014:405—420.
27. Rosen L. High tech, high touch: why technology enhances patient-centered care. In: Huffpost, ed. *The Blog*; December 13, 2012. Available from: https://www.huffingtonpost.com/lawrence-rosen-md/health-care-technology_b_2285712.html.

INDEX

'*Note:* Page numbers followed by "f" indicate figures, "t" indicate tables.'

T

U

V

W

FSC
www.fsc.org
MIX
Papier | Fördert
gute Waldnutzung
FSC® C083411

Kolibri 360 GmbH
Ferdinand-Jühlke-Straße 7
99095 Erfurt, Deutschland
produktsicherheit@kolibri360.de